A Pa...
Tee... ...ults

by
Larry E. Dumont, M.D.
and
Richard I. Altesman, M.D.

This book is not intended to replace personal medical care and supervision; there is no substitute for the experience and information that your doctor can provide. Rather, it is our hope that this book will provide additional information to help people understand the nature of cults and psychiatric conditions.

Proper medical care should always be tailored to the individual patient. If you read something in this book that seems to conflict with your doctor's instructions, contact your doctor. Your doctor may have medically sound reasons for recommending treatment that may differ from the information presented in this book.

If you have any questions about any treatment in this book, consult your doctor.

In addition, the patient names and cases used in this book do not represent actual people, but are composite cases drawn from several sources.

THE FACTS ABOUT STONY LODGE HOSPITAL

Stony Lodge Hospital is a 61-bed, private psychiatric hospital which provides effective, caring treatment—and 24-hour emergency services—to individuals and families throughout Westchester County and the surrounding Tri-State area.

As a state-of-the-art provider of psychiatric evaluation and treatment, Stony Lodge Hospital has a strong commitment to serving individuals experiencing psychiatric and dual-diagnosis (psychiatric-chemical dependency) problems. We believe our responsibility extends beyond serving patients in the hospital, to serving the community.

As a community service, we offer you the opportunity to call on our staff to serve as speakers, discussion leaders, or panel members at school, community, professional meetings or other functions.

STONY LODGE PROGRAMS INCLUDE:

The Neuropsychiatric Evaluation Program—a unique service specializing in comprehensive evaluations.

The Adolescent Psychiatric Treatment Program—a separate, structured setting tailored to the develomental, social, psychological and biological needs of adolescent patients.

The Adult Program—a supportive environment in which an intensive milieu provides individual and group psychotherapy and family therapy, coordinated with activities, and other therapies.

The Adolescent Dual-Diagnosis Program—a specialized unit devoted to treating adolescents whose psychiatric problems are complicated by alcohol or substance abuse.

The Adult Dual-Diagnosis Program—specifically designed to treat both the psychiatric and chemical dependency problems experienced by the adult patient.

Anxiety and Obsessive-Compulsive Disorders Program.

STONY LODGE HOSPITAL
P.O. Box 1250
Briarcliff Manor, NY 10510
(914) 941-7400

DEDICATION

To my parents who, in their love, put me through medical school, and therefore made this book possible.

—Larry Dumont, M.D.

To my family, former teachers, and patients, without whom this book would never have been possible.

—Richard Altesman, M.D.

ACKNOWLEDGMENTS

I would like to thank the pedagogues responsible for making me a psychiatrist: Dan Winstead, Donald Gallant, and Ake Mattsson. And a final thanks to M.G., my own personal therapist.

—Larry Dumont, M.D.

To the professionals, police, and youth officers who have been dealing with cults and their members.

—Richard Altesman, M.D.

We are especially indebted to Ron Schaumburg, whose impressive talents, professionalism and dedication made this book a reality.

In addition, we must acknowledge the research contributions of the outstanding book, *Cults and New Religious Movements*, edited by Marc Galanter, (American Psychiatric Association, 1989). This work is discussed extensively in several places throughout our book.

TABLE OF CONTENTS

1

UPDATE: THE NEWS FROM THE CULT FILE

Few things frighten parents so much as the thought that their children will be stolen from them, sucked into a vortex of evil, and transformed into unthinking zombies at the hands of a deranged psychotic. Charles Manson, the Jonestown tragedy, Satanism, heavy metal music, and "Moonies" are just a few of the thoughts associated with the word *cult*.

What is a cult? According to the dictionary, a cult is simply any group of people who follow a particular system of belief. Actually, even the founding fathers of the United States or the twelve disciples of Jesus would fit this broad criterion. The word cult derives from a Latin term meaning "to till the soil," and many cult leaders have an uncanny knack of spotting fertile ground— vulnerable young people seeking direction and meaning in their lives. Different cults hold different beliefs, and use a variety of tactics to attract and retain members. Some cults are religious in orientation; others political; still others "therapeutic."

Regardless of their different orientations, the word cult almost always invokes images of extreme horror or outrageous behavior. This association is understandable, considering the sensationalistic nature of most news stories on cults:

- The reports emanating from the steaming jungle of Guyana over a decade ago seemed too bizarre to believe: Over 900 people in the village of Jonestown, disciples of a probably psychotic madman named Jim Jones, drank cyanide-laced Kool-Aid in a mass ritual of suicide. The pictures of the bloated, rotting corpses lying in the tropical sun horrified the world.

- In 1986, less than eight years after Jonestown, a woman led nearly a thousand members of a cult called the Church Universal and Triumphant from California to a ranch in Montana. The leader, Elizabeth Clare Prophet, alias "Guru Ma," claims that she receives messages from Jesus and Buddha. And what do these messages say? Simply that the world will soon be destroyed in a nuclear holocaust. Today, Ma and her children busily prepare for Armageddon by building bomb shelters and tunnels, and by gathering enough semiautomatic weapons to equip a small army.

- A California teenager kills himself while listening to an ear-splitting brand of rock music known as heavy metal. The title of the song: "Suicide Solution."

- A 14-year-old Boy Scout stabs his mother to death, tries to burn his father and brother, then kills himself by slashing his wrists and throat. A note found in his bedroom reveals that he planned to commit these acts— including his suicide— out of worship for Satan.

Despite the tendency to lump all cults together, we must make a distinction between *destructive* and *benign* cults. A benign cult can be defined as a group of people sharing a system of belief, in which individual members do not lose their independence or autonomy. It is the destructive cults, with their harmful effects upon both the individual and the family, that will be the focus of this book. Participation in a destructive cult produces harmful changes in an individual's behavior or personality: social withdrawal, poor performance at school or on the job, and so on. There are a few traits common to most destructive cults.

First, in order to survive, cults need members. Once they have them, they need to hold on to them. Second, leaders must monitor members' thoughts and actions every moment of every day to make sure the group's philosophy has penetrated and is being put into practice. Third, cults must defend themselves against attack from "outsiders." The emotional and physical effort a cult must exert to meet these needs—plus the constant need for money to fuel the cult's ventures—can very easily lead to dangerous situations.

Consider these events, ripped from the pages of newspapers and magazines over the last few years:

- Eleven members of a back-to-nature cult known as MOVE are killed as police firebomb their headquarters in a Philadelphia row house. As firemen stand by, the fire spreads, destroying 61 homes and leaving 250 neighborhood residents homeless.
- Women members of a Hare Krishna commune in the south are beaten with a rubber hose for failing to work hard enough at panhandling. One Krishna devotee, reportedly about to blow the whistle on the commune's rampant drug smuggling and child abuse practices, is murdered in his van.
- Bhagwan Shree Rajneesh, a tiny man with piercing eyes and a fleet of nearly 100 Rolls-Royce automobiles, draws thousands of followers to a tiny town in Oregon. Within a few years, amid allegations of gun running, drug dealing, and murder, he is led away in chains to jail; his American empire crumbles, and he flees to his native India.
- L. Ron Hubbard, a science fiction writer described by his ex-wife as "hopelessly insane," invents a religion and dubs it "Scientology." Within a few decades he has enough money to qualify as a high-ranking member of the *Forbes Magazine* 400.
- The Sullivanians, a psychotherapy "cult" in New York City, have been accused of controlling the living arrangements, professional lives, finances, marriages, even the sexual

practices of 200 "patients." According to these accusations, sleeping alone is considered "an act of hostility," and members are required to sleep with a different group member every night.

SATANISM

The most chilling trend of recent years is the rise of Satanism. Nearly every day newspapers carry stories that would serve as plots for horror movies, but are in reality evidence of humanity's fascination with the power of the occult.

Our tendency at first is to dismiss such stories as isolated incidents. We want to believe that the rise in Satanism is no more than a momentary throwback to medieval times. We tell ourselves that the slavish devotion of hundreds of people to the demented vision of a powerful leader is nothing more than a fluke.

However, as the frequent and disturbing reports of murder, suicide, and Satanism show, the spell of Satanism persists.

- The man convicted of killing 13 people in Los Angeles—known as the "Night Stalker"—forced some of his victims to worship Satan before he murdered them. During his trial he stands up and shouts "Hail Satan!" As he is led away following sentencing, he flashes photographers an evil grin—and make a devil-worship sign with his fingers.
- An executive of a large corporation leads a double life as a priest in a satanic sect, using company funds to pay for his rituals.
- A voodoo cult in Mexico kidnaps American students off the streets, chops up their bodies, and boils them in a fiendish ritualistic brew.
- A 16-year-old boy writes an essay for his English class in which he states, "Satanism made me a better person. I am free. I can kill without remorse." That very night he dons a black hooded cape, pours blood on an altar in his bedroom, and assassinates his sleeping parents.

After reading these horrific reports, who could fault parents for asking . . .

"ARE CULT MEMBERS 'CRAZY'?"

Does the fact that psychiatrists have written this book mean that cult membership is a form of mental illness?

No. People who join cults are not necessarily severely psychiatrically disturbed. Some well-adjusted people—intelligent, highly educated, financially secure, from stable family backgrounds—may be drawn to a cult's philosophy because it promises spiritual rewards or the opportunity for personal growth. Despite their faults, cults can provide structure and discipline, giving focus to otherwise unfocused lives.

As psychiatrists and physicians who have treated hundreds of young people over the years, we are keenly aware that the stress of the maturing process—the discovery of sexuality, the pressures of the onset of adulthood—produces overwhelming emotional strain. For some individuals, cult membership becomes a way of expressing, and thus relieving, this turmoil.

However, prior to becoming involved with a cult, a certain percentage of teenagers do exhibit some of the symptoms of mental disorder: depression, low self-esteem, substance abuse—even hallucinations, and so on. Some meet the criteria for one or more recognized conditions, such as a mood or personality disorder, conduct or attention-deficit disorder, or antisocial behavior. Sometimes these symptoms can be so severe as to drive the person to seek relief through unusual channels, including cult affiliation. The danger is that taking part in cult activities may push a vulnerable kid over the edge, worsen these already existing traits, and lead to a full-blown psychiatric illness. That's why prevention is so important, and why aggressive intervention is called for when prevention fails.

In addition to prevention and intervention, parents should understand the impact of cults upon the family. Cults often induce members to disown their parents and run away. A cult may threaten many of the family's assets—not just money or possessions, but its values and its dreams for the child's future.

Parents who discover—or even suspect—that their child is involved in a cult feel frightened and confused. They are torn between their desire to shelter the child from harm and their wish to grant him the freedom to live his own life and make his own choices.

HEAVY METAL MUSIC

One important concern of many parents is whether to give their children the unrestricted freedom to listen to rock music, especially the genre known as "heavy metal." They worry whether such music may be doing any damage—not damage to the eardrums, although there is plenty of evidence of that. No, they fear the impact of the apparent satanic overtones of the heavy metal world.

Since the days of Elvis, rock and roll has always been a form of rebellion. Many of today's parents were heavily influenced by the popular music of the 1960s, with its messages of social revolution and protest. Part of rock's appeal to youngsters has always been the fact that it gives them an identity unique from their parents.

But heavy metal music arouses other anxieties in mom and dad. Even the names of the groups are sinister: Black Sabbath, Megadeth, Poison, Queensryche, White Snake, Slayer. The music is unrelentingly loud, featuring crashing chords and pounding drums. The lyrics—when they can be understood—seem to glorify violence (especially violence against women), hatred, and sexually deviant behavior. Of special concern are the song's occult and satanic messages. Some of the song titles from current heavy metal albums include: "Hells Bells," "Back in Black," "Shoot to Kill," "Shout at the Devil," "Necrophiliac," "Number of the Beast," "Devil's Daughter," "Hell Awaits," "Bloodbath in Paradise." What happened to the harmony and understanding that were promised in "The Age of Aquarius" two decades ago?

Some parents and experts feel that such music aggravates their kids' problems, including their use of illicit drugs. Some police and professionals see a connection between heavy metal and some cases of murder or suicide. But is there any scientific evidence that listening to "head-banging" music leads to such behavior, including cult involvement?

One study found that nearly 75 percent of adolescents hospitalized for conduct disorders involving violence preferred heavy metal music over other genres such as country and pop. Nearly 60 percent of the kids with a chemical dependency problem likewise made heavy metal their first choice. According to the researchers, "The attraction of heavy metal music is its message that a higher power controls the world, and that youngsters can sink their teeth into this philosophy, so they crank up the music, tattoo or carve in their body a symbol of Satan, and do drugs, all of which makes them feel powerful and in charge. . . . heavy metal music provides simple answers to complex problems."

But does listening to this music actually cause otherwise healthy teens to use drugs or become violent or take part in satanic rituals? In our experience, no. There are many well-functioning teens who listen to the same music. Heavy metal music must be seen within the context of your teenager's overall mental health. For the normal teenager, functioning well at home and in school, heavy metal music poses no special problems. In most cases they won't be compelled to rush out and join a satanic cult simply because they've listened to the latest heavy metal album. Our advice to parents is not to be too concerned about your teen's choice of music, *unless* your child has shown signs of an underlying psychiatric problem (such as falling grades, violent behavior, substance abuse, changes in appetite, etc.), or becomes obsessed with the music.

Psychiatrically-troubled adolescents may be drawn to heavy metal music because it expresses their inner turmoil. For these troubled teens, this music may worsen their condition, or it may undermine any therapy the child receives. For these reasons many treatment facilities may limit or even prohibit heavy metal music. The mental health and future well-being of a troubled teenager is simply too valuable to risk.

However, parents of these psychiatrically troubled adolescents should not focus exclusively on heavy metal music. Smashing all his albums won't do anything to address the underlying problems—depression, drugs, antisocial behavior—that are the *real* cause for concern, as we'll see later in this book.

ARE PARENTS TO BLAME?

If your child is involved in a cult, you as parents are probably asking yourself, "Are we to blame?" You may feel that you somehow failed in your duty to educate your children, to foster healthy values, and to provide them with a solid religious background.

The fortunate misfortune is that you are not to blame. Having worked with dozens of families, we know that kids can be drawn to cults whether they come from stable or broken homes, whether they are well-off or poor, whether they have been brought up in an established religion or not. Rigorous sociological studies demonstrate, and our own experience convinces us, that there is no "sin of omission" by parents that leads—or pushes—their children into the clutches of a cult.

Our aim is to help parents recognize the danger signals that may indicate whether their child is prone to cult influence, or indeed has already begun to dabble in cult activities. Such awareness can enable parents to prevent their child from becoming a victim of a cult. Because prevention sometimes fails, we will also outline the options parents have for rescuing their loved one—options that range from gentle persuasion to inpatient treatment at a psychiatric hospital.

The only time the question of "fault" comes into play is when the parents fail to educate themselves about the dangers of cults and ignore the signs warning them that their child is a potential victim. Reading this book acknowledges your concern, and that is the first step in circumventing tragedy.

2

WHAT IN GOD'S NAME IS GOING ON?

We humans are born with a biological urge to associate with one another. Banding together is not merely a pleasant way of passing time. As a species we have a better chance of survival if we pool our resources. Thus the powerful impulse to associate with others of "like-mindedness" usually works for our own good.

In all societies, past and present, there are people whose needs are not met by associating with the social institutions existing at the time. These people seek satisfaction outside the mainstream of their culture. Often they are motivated by their quest for spirituality. They seek a closer union with God, and feel constrained by the tenets of established religions.

The American myth holds that the nation was founded on the principles of religious freedom and tolerance. In reality, however, the first colonizers, the Puritans, were a Christian cult that demanded strict adherence to its rules. Anyone who failed to obey was cast out. A clergyman named Roger Williams, not pure enough for the Puritans, was ostracized. He left to start his own cultic commune in Rhode Island. Williams' group evolved into the Baptists—now, of course, a major denomination, but one which began as a tiny cult.

A book on depression published in 1621 described the Puritan cultists as suffering from a condition known as religious melancholia. A century later the Methodists, who broke away from the Anglican church, were similarly considered to be victims of "religious insanity." By the mid-1800s, religious insanity—the fourth most common diagnosis at the time—was thought to be "more dangerous than yellow fever or cholera."

Groups that were considered to be cults at some time in their history include Roman Catholics, Jehovah's Witnesses, Mennonites, Christian Scientists, Quakers, Mormons, Orthodox Jews, Born-Again Christians—even the computer giant IBM!

We've touched on the history of cults merely to show how yesterday's minority movement may become tomorrow's mainstream. New ideas are often threatening. But just because people embrace a strange new idea or a different philosophy does not automatically mean they are insane or dangerous—or wrong.

THE MODERN CULT

Cults are by no means a recent phenomenon. But the cults we discuss in this book have a different pedigree than the religious movements prior to 1900. In fact, three out of four current American cults sprang up after 1950. One major exception, however, is Satanism. Devil worship has been around for thousands of years, although "modern" Satanism began as an occult revival in the 1890s.

Broadly speaking, modern cults emerged as an offshoot of the social movements of the 1950s and 1960s. In rebelling against the establishment, many young people experimented with drugs, sexual freedom, or exotic philosophies, hoping to gain new insights or achieve personal transformation. Some thought the answer lay in communal living; others turned to gurus from the East.

In the 1970s, the trend shifted somewhat. Psychedelic drugs lost some of their appeal; radical political movements burned themselves out. From this social climate emerged groups with a more religious focus. Sun Myung Moon, a Korean who claimed that Jesus had appeared and told him to complete his mission, began recruiting members for his Unification Church (often called the "Moonies"). The Hare Krishna movement combed college campuses looking for recruits and in the process metamorphosed young students into devotees willing to shave their heads and chant for hours upon end. An Eastern cult known as the Divine Light Mission, led by an 8-year-old "perfect master," attracted many followers.

Naturally, parents became alarmed when their children took up with these organizations. Many such groups, sometimes known as New Religious Movements, required their members to live in communal housing and to have little or no contact with their families. Members were sometimes ordered to spend long hours aggressively panhandling or selling flowers and candy. Some members reportedly dunned their parents for contributions or stole property to meet leaders' demands. Concerned that their children had been kidnapped and brainwashed against their wills, some parents struck back by forcibly abducting their children and subjecting them to intensive "deprogramming."

A NEW AGE DAWNS

Near the end of the decade, the Jonestown horror helped take a lot of the steam out of such movements (but not all, as Guru Ma shows). New Religious Movements generally declined in number and strength. In their place, the "New Age" dawned.

New Age cults represent an unlikely blend of mysticism, self-improvement, the occult, psychotherapy, reincarnation, and paganism. It seems the New Age has room to accommodate just about any idea, no matter how quirky or out-of-this-world.

Colorado has been called the center of the New Age universe.

In Boulder, for example, twenty thousand residents—a quarter of that city's population—have undergone some kind of New Age cult training. Such training qualifies them to become "psychic reprogrammers," "life and growth empowerment practitioners," "specialists in balancing and aligning energies," "past-life regression experts," "neuro-linguistic programmers," "crystal healers," "teachers of planetary ascension," "soul mergers," or "channelers who commune with the dead." One accountant even lists "rebirthing" as one of his qualifications.

Many New Age notions have a certain naive charm. For some people, however, dabbling in mysticism may provide the first glimpse into the dark world of Satanism. Adolescents are especially vulnerable to the appeal of the supernatural. Without mature intellectual and emotional resources they may sense that they lack control over their world. They may feel afraid, and fear may make them susceptible to any huckster who promises personal power. At any moment, some event— the lyrics of a rock song, a compelling image in a rock video, an offhand remark by a friend—can propel a youngster in an unexpected direction. For today's teens, the New Age may be the beginning of the Dark Age.

CULTS: A CLOSER LOOK

Because cults by nature are eccentric, it's hard to pin down an exact definition or to identify the traits they share in common.

According to cult expert David Halperin, most cults are groups organized for the purpose of venerating an authoritarian, usually self-proclaimed leader. This leader claims to have a special relationship with God or with some other supernatural force, a relationship that imbues him or her with special powers.

We like Dr. Halperin's definition because it identifies the *leader* as the driving force behind many cults, not its philosophy. Of course, individual members may join because they embrace the cult's ideas, but often the cult itself was created to gratify the leader's need for adoration or power.

Bear in mind that a cult leader need not be present, or even alive for that matter. The founder of the Hare Krishna movement died in 1977, but the movement continues to operate out of eleven temples, each run by a different guru who operates independently. Sun Myung Moon lived in Korea but controlled followers in America, even determining who would marry whom from 10,000 miles away. And while some Satanic cult groups have High Priests or Priestesses, others are run as a kind of occult democracy, with no leader except the image of Satan himself.

Most modern cults, however, center on an individual with a powerful personality. Some experts refer to cults as "charismatic groups" to underscore the leader's magnetic character. Jim Jones, Guru Ma, Bhagwan Rajneesh, and Charles Manson are all examples of charismatic leaders.

CULTS VS. RELIGIONS

As we mentioned, some cults "grow up" to become full-fledged mainstream religions. What, then, is the distinction between a cult and a religion? Again, the focus is on the leadership of the cult. According to Dr. Louis West, cults are usually run in an authoritarian way; leaders not only suggest rules of behavior, they also actively enforce them. Usually a cult's value system is based on money, power, or the glorification of the leaders, rather than humane concerns or spiritual enrichment. Cults may also value the unorthodox behavior of their members.

Religious practices may have mystical elements, but the rituals are carried out in public. A cult, by contrast, practices its rites in secret. Cults guard their boundaries—the line between themselves and the rest of society—with fierce intensity. The boundaries are so strong that members of some cults, such as the People's Temple, would rather die than be "infected" by contact with the outside world. Cults also strictly limit the flow of information—from the outside in and from the inside out—while a church relies on open communication between itself, its members, and the society within which it operates.

Religion attempts to co-exist with the culture in which it operates. A cult rejects and withdraws from that same culture.

Sometimes religious dissenters, unhappy with the direction their church is heading, will break off and form a sect. Sects are different from cults, however. Sect members still participate in society and embrace its culture. Their only battle is with the dogma of their religion. Again, cults divorce themselves completely from the mainstream of society.

Are all communes cults? No. Communes generally have no leader. Nor are they likely to have some kind of manifesto—a book, for example—that spells out the rules and philosophy by which all members must live. The boundaries of a commune are looser; people can come and go as they like.

GOOD CULTS AND BAD

We've discussed the differences between cults and other types of religious groups. How, then, can we distinguish destructive cults from harmless ones?

The only way is to look at the impact of the cult on the individual members, families, and the community. Studies of cults show that the more totalitarian the cult's leaders are, the more likely the cult will be harmful. According to Dr. West, a totalitarian cult is one that uses unethical, manipulative, or coercive techniques of persuasion and control. Such techniques include isolating members from former friends and family, group pressure, control of access to information, promoting total dependency on the group, and so on.

Individual members may suffer at the hands of cult leadership. Abuse takes two forms: physical and psychological. Documented examples of physical abuse by cults include beatings, torture, starvation, lack of food or medical care, and forced prostitution. Psychological abuse involves isolation from

Definition of a Destructive Cult*

As these traits accumulate, the more destructive the cult will be:

1. Use of Brainwashing Techniques
- **Control** of the members' internal and external environments
- **Mystic manipulation**, including staging events that are interpreted as examples of the group's divine or perfect teachings
- **Demand for purity**, dividing everything into good and evil
- **Misuse of confession** for the sake of controlling the confessor
- **Sacred science**, a central doctrine claiming to be a perfect logical, scientific, philosophical, political, or religious system
- **Language**, including use of special terms only the group can define; replacing free thought with cult thinking, phrases, clichés
- **Valuing doctrine over people**, giving primacy to cult teachings over individual experience
- **Control of life and death**, assuming power over who may exist

2. Misuse of Mind-Altering Techniques
Such as when chanting, praying, meditating, hypnosis, speaking in tongues, or repetitive actions (counting beads, reciting, rereading the same passage) are used to control or brain-wash the individual.

3. Deception
Misleading recruits about the group's purpose, beliefs, goals, activities, history, leadership.

4. Authoritarian Structure
Dominated by a leader or group of leaders who refuse to accept responsibility for any wrongdoing. No means of

recourse within the group. Rejection of all criticism from outside agencies. Faults and errors of the group are attributed to misperception by members, not to flaws in the group's principles.

---

*Adapted with permission from "Working Definition of a Destructive Cult," published by the Cult Awareness Network of New York and New Jersey, who wishes to acknowledge chapter 22 of R.J. Lifton's *Thought Reform and the Psychology of Totalism: A study of brain-washing in China.* W.W. Norton, 1966.

the outside society, "shunning" by other members of the cult, emotional deprivation (as when children are taught not to cry), and mind control techniques, including constant indoctrination and the absence of free thought.

To our way of thinking, any group that abuses its members physically or psychologically, or that interferes with family functioning—separating parents from the children, controlling marriages and sexual relationships, and so on—qualifies as a destructive cult. Period. A list of "the evil that cults do" appears in the Box on page 15.

How Cults Hurt*

1. Individuals and Families

- Mental or emotional illness; impaired psychological development; physical disease, injury, or death of cult members.
- Fragmentation of families
- Financial exploitation of members and their families
- Neglect and abuse of children, including deaths resulting from physical violence, profound neglect, or the denial of medical treatment

2. Government and Law

- Infiltration of government agencies, political parties, community groups, and military organizations for the purpose of obtaining classified or private informa-

tion, gaining economic advantage, or influencing the infiltrated organizations to serve the ends of the cult
- Tax evasion
- Fraudulent acquisition and illegal disposition of public assistance and social security funds
- Violation of immigration laws
- Abuse of the legal system through spurious lawsuits, groundless complaints to licensing and regulatory bodies, or extravagant demands for governmental or legal services
- Pursuit of political goals while operating under the rubric of a nonpolitical, charitable, or religious organization

3. *Business*
- Deceptive fund-raising and selling practices
- Organizational and individual stress resulting from pressuring employees to participate in cultic "management training" and "growth seminars"
- Misuse of charitable status in order to secure money for business and other noncharitable purposes
- Unfair competition through the use of underpaid labor or "recycled salaries" by cult-operated enterprises

4. *Education*
- Denial of, or interference with, legally required education of children in cults
- Misuse of schools or college facilities, or misrepresentation of the cult's purposes, in order to gain respectability
- Recruitment of college students through violation of their privacy or deception, often with subsequent disruption of such students' educational programs or goals

5. *Religion*
- Attempts to gain the support of established religions by presenting a deceptive picture of the cult's goals, beliefs, and practices; and seeking to make "common cause" of various issues
- Infiltration of established religious groups in order to recruit members into the cult

---

*From a seminar on cultism sponsored by the American Family Foundation, the Neuropsychiatric Institute of UCLA, and the Johnson Foundation, September 9–11, 1985.

SOME CULT DEMOGRAPHICS

Who joins cults? There are so many different types of cults around, and so little research, that it's hard to say. However, a study of a small group of people who joined cults (including the Unification Church, Scientology, the Divine Light Mission, and Hare Krishna, among others) found that the average age of a cult member at the time of joining was 21.5 years. Sixty percent were male; all were Caucasian. Half came from Protestant backgrounds, a fifth were Jewish, and the rest Catholic. Typically they came from middle-income families, attended college, and had a B grade average. Such figures don't tell the whole tale, but they give us some indication.

How widespread are cults? No one knows. Estimates of the number of cults currently operating in this country range from 500 to 5,000. The American Family Foundation, a research and educational group devoted to the study of cults, suggests there are at least a thousand cults in the United States and Europe. Cult experts Joan Carol Ross and Michael D. Langone estimate that perhaps as many as one million Americans—one out of every 250 people—have been involved with a cult sometime during the last twenty years.

The figures vary, depending on which part of the country you're looking at. In San Francisco, for example, 3 percent of people surveyed reported that they belonged to a cult, while half of those between the ages of 18 and 30 indicated they would accept an invitation to attend a cult meeting. Police in Richmond, Virginia estimate that an astounding 8 percent of the population may be involved in Satanic worship at some level! Satanic cults or groups that parody the Christian religion may be more common in areas where Christianity is strong, such as certain parts of the South. White supremacist or survivalist cults, like Guru Ma's Church Universal and Triumphant, seem to prefer the wilderness areas in the Northwest. On a personal level, our hospitals, located in New Jersey and New York, have experienced an increase in adolescent patients with a history of Satanic involvement.

There are cults to suit every taste (see the Appendix for

more information). Religious cults run the gamut from Satanism and voodoo to Pentecostals who become so filled with the Holy Spirit that they writhe on the floor and speak in tongues. There are fundamentalist (Born Again) groups that advocate strict adherence to the Bible, while other groups rewrite the Bible as needed to reinforce their beliefs.

The other main group of religious cults espouse variations on Hindu philosophy and include the followers of Bhagwan Rajneesh, the Hare Krishnas, and the Divine Light Mission.

Such groups as Radical Loyalty (their motto: "It's great to be white!") and Christians Awake are less religious and more political in their orientation. And some cults are neither religious nor political but are founded on therapeutic concepts. Examples include L. Ron Hubbard's Scientology, the Sullivanians, and the Forum, an offshoot of the Erhard Seminars Training, or "est," movement of the 1970s.

FACTORS IN THE RISE OF CULTS

How can so many cults spring up, attract members, and thrive? As we've said, humans are biologically bound to associate with each other. We are compelled to form communities. But what is it about our modern society that fails to satisfy the needs of so many of its members? Why do some people feel they must look outside traditional institutions for the answers they seek?

One way to look at the question is to ask if there is anything *good* about cults. Do cults simply attract people who are evil or antisocial? Or do they have something to offer those who are sincerely searching for a path to enlightenment? Is cult membership the disease or the cure? And can it be both?

How is this possible? Investigators who have explored that question from many angles find that joining groups, especially religious groups, can enhance one's sense of self, improve family relationships, or in some cases strengthen ties to the community.

Perhaps another clue to the rise in modern cults lies in the point we made earlier: that 75 percent of modern cults arose after 1950. The nuclear explosions that ended World War II dramatized the power we have to destroy ourselves. The fear of sudden annihilation—never before so real—leads some people to mistrust the ability of government or established religions to provide protection. They turn to other sources for help, following Jim Jones into the jungle or Guru Ma to Montana to escape Armageddon.

Others join cults searching for some higher notion to satisfy their spiritual thirst. Of course, someone stranded in the desert will drink any water, no matter how brackish.

The social experiments of the 1960s—particularly the use of illicit drugs—also contributed to the rise of cults. Many users of mind-altering drugs, such as marijuana and LSD, felt that they had seen glimpses of a deeper reality. When they discovered cult leaders who also professed to have special insight into that reality, they were more inclined to follow. The cult represented another possible road to Ultimate Awareness.

ROLE OF THE FAMILY

The need to associate with other people, the decline of spiritualism, the specter of nuclear war, substance abuse—all contributed to the emergence of cult behavior. But some authorities feel that more important than all of these put together is the breakdown of the basic family unit.

The high divorce rate results in more families who are led by a single parent. With one parent missing, the other must not only provide for the family but manage the home as well. There is little time to devote to the psychic needs of all family members. Without support and encouragement from parents, children may develop a warped sense of values, or no values at all. Such children are at risk of developing in a cultural vacuum.

One police investigator stated bluntly, "I feel we wouldn't have to investigate occult crimes if it wasn't for the breakdown of America's family structure. We believe we have many youths involved in the occult today because of their broken families."

Although family schism may be a factor, not everyone who joins a cult or dabbles in the occult comes from a broken home. On the contrary, many are raised by both parents and are financially well off.

This important fact led a sociologist named Neil Maron to investigate how the family environment contributes to a child's decision to join a cult. Before his study, he made several predictions about what he would find. He thought that, compared to normal families, those with a son or daughter involved in a cult would prove to be more enmeshed—that is, the parents would have high expectations of achievement for their offspring and would be overly involved in their children's lives. He also thought parents would have a higher incidence of mental disorders, including depression and alcoholism. Such families, he guessed, probably placed less value on moral or religious training and more on intellectual or cultural achievement.

Wrong on all counts! To his surprise, not one of his predictions was borne out by the facts. Families whose offspring joined cults were virtually indistinguishable from other families. The emphasis on morality and intellectual achievement, incidence of mental illness—none of these factors had any impact on in the child's vulnerability to cult involvement. Maron did find, however, that kids who joined cults had fewer close friendships, fewer romantic involvements, less alcohol use (!), and less religious training. And in our practice, we find that teenagers who become involved in Satanism do tend to come from more disrupted families than those who join the types of cults considered in this study.

The bottom line: A child's decision to join a cult does not arise because the parents somehow failed in their duty. It doesn't matter if the parents are divorced, if they drink too much, if they dote on their children or neglect them. In many cases, the family is not a significant factor in the child's susceptibility to cults. Vulnerability arises for other reasons, as we'll explain in Chapter 4.

If you are blaming yourself for your child's actions, such blame is not only misplaced, it's unproductive. Agonizing over the question of "Where did we go wrong" does nothing but drain the energy you need to address the *real* issue: What do we do now?

The next step is to assess the level of your child's cult involvement. In the following chapter we will discuss the warning signs you need to watch for.

3

WARNING SIGNS: IS MY KID ONE OF THEM?

- A 13-year-old boy shows up for breakfast one Sunday morning bearing a tattoo in the shape of a pentagram on his arm.
- A high school senior suddenly begins to sprinkle her conversation with strange terms and words that hold meaning only to her.
- On a family visit during Thanksgiving break, a college freshman announces he has dropped out of school to devote more time to "finding himself."

What's happening here? Did the boy get the tattoo simply because he thought it was "cool," or was it part of some Satanic initiation rite? Does the girl's speech show she is the victim of brainwashing? Does the college student's sudden shift in direction simply mean he wasn't ready to leave home, or has he fallen in with a group who is making other plans for him?

As doctors, we know that a single symptom isn't enough to

make a diagnosis. Tracing the broader *pattern* of symptoms reveals the problem. The same is true when trying to figure out if someone has fallen prey to a cult. Knowing whether the child is merely flirting with bizarre notions or has actually enlisted in a movement is crucial in determining what type of intervention—if any—is needed.

In this chapter we'll point out some of the emotional and behavioral changes that people who take up with cults, including Satanism, often exhibit. We'll also note some of the other possible causes for those changes.

THE CULT PREDISPOSITION

There is no single personality profile, no list of characteristics, that we can point to and say with certainty, *"This* is someone who will wind up in a cult." However, we can identify certain traits that may *predispose* a person to cult involvement. Predisposition simply means that a person may be prone to leaning a certain way. A gentle pull in another direction at the right time can prevent disaster.

Naiveté

People who are naive lack the perception or intuitive judgment that would help them live in the real world. Almost by definition, young adolescents are naive. They haven't had the time or experience to develop a repertoire of responses to life's many challenges, nor they made enough mistakes to know which of their judgments are faulty and which are sound. As a result they may prefer a simple answer, or a dramatic one. Many cults promise exactly that.

Idealism

Idealists measure the world by the yardstick of perfection. They expect other people and events to meet impossible standards of excellence. The idealist is let down when a teacher says "I don't know" or when a parent makes an error.

Such people would naturally be drawn to a cult leader who, for example, claims to be an infallible Perfect Master.

Ignorance

Ignorance is not the same thing as stupidity—the inability to learn. It means simply the lack of knowledge. If an adolescent isn't told of the dangers of cults, he or she may remain ignorant about their dangers—until it is too late.

Situational Stress

Because adolescents lack perspective, a momentary glitch in life may seem like the end of the world. The breakup of a teen's love affair may be one of a dozen he or she will experience over the course of a lifetime. But because it is the first and so far the only such tragedy, it is exquisitely painful. Other examples of stress include school problems, feelings of failure, death of a friend or relative, trouble finding or keeping a job, illness, and relocation. For someone under stress, a cult's simplistic promises of relief may have overwhelming appeal.

Dependency

By this we don't mean chemical dependency, but over-reliance on other people. Teens who can't function happily on their own, who constantly turn to their friends or their family for stimulation or entertainment, or even identity, are susceptible to anyone who promises to satisfy all their needs.

Excessively Trusting Nature

Note the word "excessively." We must all trust others at some time in our lives. *Excessive* trust means surrendering all critical judgment and personality autonomy and allowing oneself to be guided by others.

Disillusionment

Naive, trusting idealists are riding for a fall. Sooner or later—usually sooner—they find the real world doesn't measure up. As they struggle to adjust to their new perception, they are likely to grab onto any new illusion that presents itself. Many cults are happy to manufacture that illusion for them.

CHANGES IN BEHAVIOR AFTER JOINING A CULT

In a sense, puberty is a form of rebirth—not just of the body but of the whole personality. Hormones switch the sexual machinery to "on." The physical onslaught of maturity, coupled with intense social pressure to adopt new roles and accept new responsibilities, leaves many kids feeling frightened. Uncertain of their identities and goals, they try out new personalities and behaviors like T-shirts, trying to find one that fits.

Behavioral changes are thus an integral part of adolescence. However, they can also be the result of cult influences. Here are some of the specific things to watch for.

Appearance

Clothes, hairstyles, and body markings are the ways people reveal their identity to the world. Sometimes the purpose of wearing a green-dyed spiked Mohawk haircut is simply to shock. Other times such styles become a kind of uniform linking individuals to a group or an ideology.

Many cults have "dress codes" that their members must follow as an outward sign of devotion. Until recently, followers of Rajneesh were asked to wear some shade of orange at all times. Some religious or therapeutic cults demand their men wear suits, ties, and short haircuts. Quasi-militaristic groups might adopt uniforms that smack of the brown shirts worn by Nazis in the 1930s. If your teenager evolves from a long-haired slob to a fastidious dresser overnight, don't panic. Adolescence is the time to explore your identity and find who you are, and parents must anticipate startling discoveries as their child makes this journey. For some adolescents, however, joining a cult is a convenient detour on this grueling trek.

Activities

Cults often encourage recruits to distance themselves from old friends and family, including spouses, and to form new partnerships with other members. You have reason to be concerned if your teenager suddenly drops out of his circle of friends and takes up with a new, totally different crowd.

The same holds of social activities. One parent told me her daughter Paula used to go and hear live rock music practically every night. Within a few weeks, however, she stopped frequenting the music clubs and announced her plan to sell off her record collection at a garage sale. Asked why, the girl replied, "I found out the devil speaks through that music."

Attitudes

Changing the way we feel about something can be a sign of growth and maturity. Usually, though, such changes come about gradually as a result of experience. Suddenly shifting to the opposite extreme, as Paula did in her attitude about music, may be a sign of trouble. Depending on the cult, a recruit may undergo a radical change in attitudes or emotional feelings about God, drugs, sex, family life, career, or the future of the universe. A member of a religious cult may reject anything having to do with the "material world"; conversely, a member of a therapeutic cult may reject everything connected to the family religion or culture. Many times happy, loving people become cold and withdrawn because they have been told to reject "earthly life" or "the chains forged by your family."

Actions

Sometimes a new cult member, unsure how his family will react, becomes secretive, refusing to state where he is going or when he'll be back. We know of one parent who became concerned when his daughter had a lock put on her bedroom door. One night when she was out of town he broke into her room. He found she had decorated her room with candles and Satanic symbols; her shelves were stuffed with books on the occult, and she had constructed a small altar beside her bed.

For some families, the tragic tipoff to cult involvement is a sudden marriage, divorce, running away from home, or relocation to another part of the country or the world. Some groups, like the Unification Church, arrange marriages, ostensibly to further the cult's principles. Sometimes, though, marriages are created solely in order to allow someone to emigrate to America.

Academic Setbacks

Cult membership can divert energy away from schoolwork. A Bible study group that meets every night and on weekends, for example, can leave little time for the study of math or English. When a bright kid's grades suddenly begin to suffer, something may be wrong.

Also, college campuses are fertile grounds for cult recruiting practices. New students especially, some of whom are away from home for the first time, are overwhelmed by their new environment, the social pressure, and the demands of schoolwork. Feeling lonely and out of place, they respond quickly to warm overtures by friendly cultists. When a young person suddenly leaves school, or abandons academic goals, the decision may be the result of cult pressure.

Lifestyle

Suddenly moving into a communal house, with the sacrifice of privacy, comfort, convenience, and even hygiene, may signal cult involvement. Cults depend on controlling their members' activities; the easiest way to do so is to have them live together. If they can't ship them to a ranch in Oregon, the next best thing is set up housekeeping somewhere in the city. The Sullivanians, for example, occupy an apartment building in New York City.

For some parents, the first clue to cult involvement is a change in the child's diet. The Hare Krishnas, like all Hindu groups, are vegetarians; some groups follow a macrobiotic diet, and so on. In most cases, a child who becomes a vegetarian or strict follower of dietary laws, is becoming his own person, and for some parents, even that is hard to digest.

Cults, like any industry, need cash to survive. The first duty of many cult members is to bring in funds. Thus a teenager who turns down a friend's invitation to play softball because he has to sell candy on a street corner may be working for some guru somewhere. In some cases a member leaves a good job to begin working for a cult enterprise, such as a newsletter. Another sign of trouble is when someone gives away large amounts of cash, or asks parents for large contributions, or perhaps abuses credit cards.

Some commercial ventures, while not exactly cults, take on some of the appearance of a cult. Any time members have left over from pushing health or home care products onto their friends is spent attending "motivational meetings" or "training seminars" on how to boost sales.

Extreme commitment in any form may be a red flag warning that a cult is operating in the vicinity.

Language

Creation of a specialized vocabulary is an important way that groups distinguish themselves from each other. Using buzzwords also serves as a means of identifying who's "in" and who's "out." (Just listen to two minutes of conversation between computer enthusiasts!)

People who have gone through a therapeutic-cult workshop may begin to talk about "centering" their lives or "catching the vision." In the notorious "est" seminars of the 1970s, participants talked of "getting it." Members of the Unification Church refer to the "Divine Principle"—which suggests that Rev. Moon is the reincarnation of Christ. The speech of Hare Krishnas is peppered with references to Govinda, Siva, and other gods of the Hindu pantheon.

It's not just words; whole speech patterns may change, which shows the impact that cult doctrine can have on thought processes. People who formerly enjoyed talking about a broad range of topics suddenly become narrowly focused. Like politicians primed before a debate, a cult member uses speech that is stuffed with stock phrases and cliches.

Well-Being

Cults have tremendous psychological as well as physical impact on their members. The pressure to learn the ways of the cult and put them into practice is intense. So rigid are their standards that fear of failing to live up to expectations or of disappointing the cult leader can wreak psychic havoc. Depending on the cult's focus, members may be converted into life-hating nihilists or into abnormally upbeat, robotic proselytizers.

Sometimes parents first notice the problem when their otherwise healthy child becomes sickly. In one instance, a mother worried because her son was unable to drag himself out of bed in the morning. Thinking he might be depressed or was having trouble in school, she talked to his classmates and found out he was spending hours each night participating in seances and other forms of witchcraft.

MARK OF THE DEVIL: THE WARNING SIGNS OF SATANISM

One night in March 1986, a bright, handsome boy summoned a demon called Ezurate to enter his body. Once possessed, he grabbed a .44 Magnum handgun and killed his parents. Earlier, in letters to a friend, he had written: "One Satanist equals ten Christians in power. Can you imagine a world dominated with our kind?... Remember, in order to get power from Satan you must earn his respect and prove yourself to him. Satan rules the earth today."

Increasingly newspapers carry reports of arson, torture,

kidnapping, animal sacrifice and murder associated with the activities of Satanic cults. What is going on? Is Satanism real, or is it just a label people have been using for centuries to denote anything mysterious or evil?

Sad to say, Satanism appears to be a growing force. The evidence is too strong to dismiss it totally as a "fad" or the result of "pranks" by a few mischievous youths. Not long ago we listened in horror as one of our patients, a 16-year-old girl, described a ritual she had observed in which a cat was ritualistically slaughtered and drained of its blood.

There are different levels of involvement in Satanism. The first level is a kind of "ad hoc," or "self-styled" Satanism—a superficial form of devil worship. A kid involved at this level responds to some Satanic image: a drawing, a song lyric, or a fantasy game like "Dungeons and Dragons" or the Ouija board. For someone in this stage, Satanism is fantasy, not a religion. The game stops when it's time to go inside for dinner, or to go to bed.

Not for everyone, though. Some people who flirt with Satanism become intrigued by its history, its mythology, its rituals and trappings. They might read a book on the subject—there are plenty to be had—and begin trying on some of the concepts for size. This is a group we call "Satanic dabblers," and are considered to be at risk. For a list of the characteristics of dabblers, see the Box on page 32.

Some kids are attracted to Satanism because it represents the ultimate form of rebellion—not just against parents, but against man, God, and the universe. "It's like the occult version of the Marines," said Linda Blood, a former Satanist. "Are you man enough for this? Do you have what it takes?" At this level, Satanism is a way of acting out hostile feelings on a grand scale.

Those most deeply involved in Satanism are known as believers. As the label suggests, they are serious about this stuff—deadly serious. They accept Satan as a true power, one who demands worship and sacrifice.

What is the evidence that a kid has taken up with the devil?

CHARACTERISTICS OF A SATANIC
JUVENILE DABBLER*

The more of these traits that apply, the greater the chance that the youngster is involved in Satanism:

1. Male, white, 14 to 20 years of age.
2. Above-average intelligence
3. Underachiever
4. Low self-esteem
5. Social outcast
6. History of substance abuse
7. Suicidal tendencies
8. Listens to heavy metal music
9. Participates in fantasy role-playing games
10. Wears black clothes and T-shirts with the names of heavy metal rock bands
11. Preoccupied with death
12. Has self-inflicted stab wounds or cigarette burns
13. Wears silver jewelry (often in occult shapes)

*Source: Cult Awareness Network—National Office

One strong clue is that he owns a copy of such books as *The Satanic Bible* by Anton LaVey, who in 1969 founded the Church of Satan. He may also keep his own "Book of Shadows," a notebook of some kind in which he jots down spells and incantations.

Satanism demands rituals. People who stumble across the scene of a Satanic ritual are often horrified by the words or symbols painted on the walls or the objects left behind. Satanic rituals are usually grotesque parodies of Christian rites. There is even a Satanic calendar listing 13 "holidays," including Halloween. Chillingly, criminal investigators report that many crimes related to Satanic practices—including kidnapping and human sacrifice—reach their peak on these days.

A common symbol of Satanism is the pentagram, a five-pointed star with one aimed at the ground (toward hell) and two points aimed skyward (like the horns of Satan). Sometimes the pentagram is enclosed in a circle (the cover of this book shows a pentagram and other symbols.) Other symbols include a goat's head (called a "baphomet"), an upside-down cross, the numbers "666," and swastikas.

Objects associated with satanic rituals include knives, bells, chalices, gongs, crucibles, incense, rock or stone altars, and candles. The color of candles is significant: black means protection from evil spirits, purple means power, and so on.

To show their loyalty, many diehard Satanists have tattoos or body markings. Commonly, such markings may be of black panthers, goat's heads, upside-down crosses, spiders, snakes, skulls, a black rose, or words such as NEMA and NATAS (amen and Satan backwards). Many wear jewelry—rings, earrings, chains—with these symbols. The jewelry is silver, since Satan seems to prefer silver.

Many parents ask us whether their teenager is a Satanist because he listens to music by rock groups such as Megadeth, AC/DC, Slayer, Motley Crue, KISS, Metallica, and so on. It is certainly true that such music is permeated with Satanic images, not just in the words but on the album jackets and in the musician's costumes. Millions of kids listen to this music, but most emerge with no more harm done than a little hearing loss. But a small percentage do take it seriously. Perhaps the safest comment to make is that not everyone who listens to heavy metal is a Satanist, but many teens involved with Satanic cults are drawn to such music because it expresses their affinity with negativism, and even violence and destruction.

This book is not the place for a detailed examination of Satanic practices. Our intention here is to mention a few of the key images that may signal involvement in a Satanic cult to alert you to the dangers.

CULT? OR SOMETHING ELSE?

A sneeze may be sparked by a viral cold, a pollen allergy, or a speck of dust. Similarly, the "symptoms" associated with cult involvement may arise from a number of other causes.

Maturity

In some cases, by the time a family comes to us for help they already know for certain that their child has taken up with a cult. In other cases, though, they may only suspect cult involvement, or even be totally ignorant of their child's association with a cult. They wonder about their son's sudden interest in a new religion, or their daughter's complete about-face in political views, or her choice to quit school and go to work full-time.

In exploring such issues, families often discover that such upheavals are the result of nothing more sinister than the process known as Growing Up. It's ironic, but the basic task of parents is to prepare their child to live independently. Sometimes parents do their work so well that their children choose to go off in a completely opposite direction. When parents in that situation ask, "Where did we go wrong?" we tell them, "You didn't do anything wrong—you succeeded admirably! You produced a free-thinking, strong-minded child who feels comfortable making decisions, acting on them, and taking responsibility for them."

Parental Hangups

Other cases are not so simple. It may turn out that the problem lies not with the child but with the parents. Some are so attached to their child that they can't let go. Conversely, a father who holds an extreme political view may feel threatened if his daughter refuses to share his opinion. Having failed to convince his own child, he accuses the girl's teachers or friends of brainwashing her against him!

If you are troubled by your child's behavior, do a little soul-searching. Are you concerned because your kid is acting independently of you? Or that he's doing something you told him not to do? Who is being hurt—you or your child? Cult authorities Joan Ross and Michael Langone suggest you ask yourself some tough questions to try to determine *exactly* what's bothering you (see Box, below). Depending on your answers, it may turn out that the problem is not with your child but with your own anxieties or fears. Discussing these issues with your child—admittedly a difficult task—may help you discover the real cause of the trouble.

Questions for Parents*

Which behavior by my child do I find upsetting?
In what ways, if any, is my child being harmed?
If there is no harm, why am I upset?
How do I feel about my child growing up?
Do I feel hurt and rejected because my child no longer needs me?
Do my child's lifestyle and values threaten or alienate me?
Am I angry or disappointed that my child isn't following the path I had in mind?
Do my hopes match my child's abilities or interests?
Are my expectations for my child realistic and healthy?

---

*Adapted from *Cults: What Parents Should Know* by Joan Carol Ross and Michael D. Langone. Weston, Mass.: American Family Foundation, 1988 and published by Lyle Stuart Books, a division of Carrol Publishing Group.

Mental Disorders

Some of the behaviors associated with cult involvement are also seen in a number of common **psychiatric** illnesses. Our experience treating troubled kids has convinced us that *participation in a cult is usually not the issue; it may be a sign of some deeper underlying emotional problem.* As psychiatrists we look beyond the immediate behavior to try and find out what is *really* going on inside the adolescent's mind. Usually, when we treat the underlying condition—depression, or an emerging thought disorder such as schizophrenia, or a personality disorder—the problem of cult involvement decreases significantly. More on this in the next chapter.

We've looked at the signs that may mean "Warning! Cult at Work!" In Chapter 4 we'll look at some of the reasons why adolescents are particularly susceptible to the lure of cults.

WHY DO KIDS
JOIN CULTS?

As the poet John Donne observed, "No man is an island, entire of itself." We are social creatures; like bees and ants, we depend on one another for survival. Our need is strongest when we are at our weakest. In times of turmoil, our natural impulse is to turn to others.

Sociologists and psychiatrists generally agree that adolescence is even more tumultuous today than in times past. Kids reach maturity at an earlier age, which fuels their desire to experiment with sex long before they are ready to handle the consequences. The same for their involvement with illicit drugs. And in today's society, life-changing decisions are being made earlier than ever: school, career, and so on. The institutions that in past decades offered support and guidance—family, church, schools—are less stable, less able to cope with the challenges of modern living. This is the generation whose parents fought in and fought against the Vietnam War, so that they were "conceived" in a cynical, uncertain world, where authority figures could no longer be relied upon, and disillusionment clouded their development.

But why do some people turn to *cults?* Why not join the Boy Scouts or the volleyball team? There is no single answer. Instead, we must consider a "formula" for cult attraction, a formula that takes into account such variables as individual personality, social pressure, and family dynamics. When these factors are mixed together in just the right proportion, the result can be a cult-vulnerable child.

INDIVIDUAL FACTORS

Physical Changes

The most obvious feature of adolescence, and in many ways the most troubling, is the complete transformation the body undergoes. Overnight, it seems, everything changes. Kids get taller, thicker, stronger. The voice changes. Sexual features grow prominent. The bones grow, but the muscles may not be able to keep up. The changes are not just external. New hormones in large doses course through the body, unleashing a flood of new feelings and emotions. Kids feel awkward (they *are* awkward!), which leads to embarrassment, which leads to even more awkwardness.

Of course, the basic biological purpose of this pubescent overhaul is to prepare the body for reproduction. But just because the sexual equipment is in place doesn't mean its owner is emotionally or intellectually prepared to use it. During the transition to adulthood, kids are pulled in many directions. Their bodies flood them with sexual signals, impelling them on to adulthood and independence. Yet adolescents lack maturity and judgment to respond to those signals. As Dr. Henry Work notes, the messages coming from our culture and its media exaggerate the image of sexuality and promote the idea of immediate gratification.

Part of the Formula of Cult Vulnerability, then, involves the teen's sense of awkwardness and insecurity, coupled with biological and cultural pressure to act on impulse. For some people, cults offer a structure within which they can channel— or suppress—those impulses.

Stress

The decision to sign on with a cult often occurs at times of personal crisis, transition, or loss. In many cases a kid who joins has recently become alienated from some other non-cult group: he may have been kicked off the basketball team or have become disenchanted with youth club meetings at his church. Still needing others, but cut off from his former crowd, he seeks to plug into some other current.

In several surveys, members of cults (and their parents) reported that they had experienced one or more highly stressful events in the previous year. Such events included the death of a close friend or relative, sickness, broken romantic relationship, loss of a job, frustration in finding a job, failure at school, extensive travel, and abrupt personality change.

Of course, these events might occur normally during the course of anyone's life. Losing one's job, for example, does not automatically mean a person will run away and join a cult. We should think of stress as just one more ingredient in the mix. Depending on other factors, the greater the number of stressful events, the more desperate the individual might be to seek relief, and the more attractive the lure of a cult might seem.

Intellectual Vulnerability

Scientist Carl Sagan wrote about an encounter with a cab driver who asked if Sagan would mind answering his questions about science. The cabbie proceeded to ask about "channeling," the healing powers of crystals and pyramids, reincarnation, and other such matters. Sagan patiently debunked each of these fields of "science." The point of Sagan's article was to decry the lack of solid factual knowledge, specifically about science, that exists in our country today. Ivan Stang, who for twenty years has studied America's cults—what he calls the "zoo of beliefs"—make a similar point: widespread ignorance creates a fertile ground in which irrational beliefs bloom and spread.

Researchers have noted that kids who have trouble in school fall into at least two groups. In one group are those who lack some of the basic intellectual tools they need to learn. As school becomes more difficult, they feel more and more left behind. It's possible for them to overcome their slow start, but not without sensitive guidance by teachers and parents. In the other group are those bright kids who are pushed onto the "fast track" by ambitious parents. These are the ones who play violin at three and solve quadratic equations at six. The danger is that these kids may burn out by the time they reach puberty, or they may be treated as more mature than they really are.

Obviously, intellectual emptiness can make one susceptible to the quirky notions peddled by religious hucksters and cultic quacks. In contrast, too much cerebral stimulation, or the assumption that a child is mature beyond his years, can drive the kid to seek relief by shutting down the brain and opting for simple, soothing answers.

Spiritual Emptiness

The quest for spiritual experience is a basic human drive. Some philosophers might even say that such a quest defines us as being human. We all want to feel that we are in touch with something beyond ourselves.

Many cult leaders announce that they have special access to God or that they possess the Secrets of the Universe. Naturally they attract people who are looking for spiritual enlightenment, especially those who feel at odds with the mainstream religions. But they also attract those individuals who have other spiritual needs, including guidance, nurture, and love. Such people turn to cults to help them define their purpose in life, to alleviate inner conflict, to exercise self-control, or discover a new source of self-esteem.

Search for Community

As Dr. Brent Wenegrat observes, the degree to which cults flourish indirectly measures how well our culture constructively meets basic human needs. One such need is to exist within a community of like-minded individuals—an in-group. Sociologists note that American society in the late twentieth century fails in many ways to create a sense of community. We move around too much; fear of strangers insulates us and prevents us from reaching out to our neighbors. We feel alienated.

According to Dr. Wenegrat, there are three main elements that fuel the drive to belong to a stable group. For one, we naturally tend to classify people as either "us" or "them." Having a recognizable "them" allows us to direct our innate hostilities away from our own group and toward our perceived enemies. Another factor is that alienation from a group produces a sense of dysphoria—anxiety, depression, restlessness. Rejoining the group, or linking up with a different group, relieves these feelings. Lastly, some people tend to accept a group's consensual view as valid, even if it conflicts directly with their personal experience.

Even people who have an ideal family life, who are intelligent, mature, and high in self-esteem seek to become members of a group. In the absence of other options, cults may appeal because they counteract the sense of alienation and replace it with a sense of communion. In a cult, or in any group for that matter, one member sees the others as self-reinforcing. The thought goes something like this: "I believe in an ideal; so does that person over there. We can't both be wrong. Therefore we must be right!" Naturally members experience a sense of bonding when they encounter others who share their view of the world. Bonding is the psychic glue that holds cults together, in spite of (perhaps even because of) opposition from outside.

Rebellion

Any parent knows that kids sometimes rebel just for the hell of it. Many times such rebellion focuses on religion.

Joining a cult movement that diametrically opposes his family's beliefs or that runs against the grain of society may be the adolescent's way of flexing his independent muscles.

Satanism has particular appeal for rebellious teens. What could be more shocking than to worship the devil and carry out his demands? What could demonstrate one's attitudes toward society more effectively than to adopt an attitude that turns the Ten Commandments upside down and violates every aspect of the Judeo-Christian heritage on which our civilization is founded? As Larry Zilliox, an investigator for the Cult Awareness Network put it, "Satanism is attractive, rebellious behavior for juveniles. Kids like it."

Personality Factors

A key element in the Formula of Vulnerability is personality. The personality—defined as a characteristic way of thinking, feeling, and acting—is the ingrained pattern of behavior that develops as we adapt, consciously and unconsciously, to stresses and changes in our environment. People with a shy personality may avoid contact with others; those with dominating personalities try to manipulate others, and so on. Here are some of the personality traits that cause certain people to be more susceptible than others to cult influence:

Low self-esteem or self-confidence. Someone who feels she is worthless or incompetent may respond when cult leaders or members shower her with attention and praise. Many cult members report that belonging to the group generates intense feelings of specialness and importance. It's a chilling fact that both Sun Myung Moon and Charles Manson (whose "family" carried out a horrifying mass murder in the late 1960s) led their followers to believe that they were among the favored converts that the Book of Revelations claimed would transform the world.

Underachievement. Among the members of many cults are some bright and talented individuals who somehow fail to find satisfying ways to develop themselves within the usual social frameworks, such as schools or hobbies. These kids perform below the level that their intelligence or ability really permits. Cults may seem attractive to an underachiever because they make fewer demands on their skills and intelligence.

Boredom. Our culture is fast-paced and fragmented. Watch any three minutes of an MTV music video and you'll see what we mean. Images flash past our eyes; random bits of sound and light assault the senses. Movies are filled with ever-more-gruesome thrills and violence. When the song is ended, when the movie is over, real life—plain old everyday life—intrudes and seems dull by comparison. Kids who crave thrills, and who may or may not have access to illicit drugs, may turn to cults for stimulation. A New Jersey public defender observes that "delinquency (that is, Satanism) is caused by total abstract boredom. It is kids looking for spiritual gratification of some kind, something mysterious."

Loneliness. We won't belabor the point, but many kids join cults simply to be with other kids. By adopting Satanic trappings, for example, or by professing strange beliefs, they indicate their oneness with other like-minded souls. Doing so alleviates their feeling that they are the only ones in the world who think and feel the way they do.

Powerlessness. Many cults, especially the self-help or therapeutic groups, are devoted to restoring to their members a sense of power over their lives. In some cases this effort can have some positive effects: Members shed their fears or inhibitions and feel inspired to realize their deepest ambitions. In other cases, though, power is seen as a way of controlling others, of exacting revenge for being downtrodden for so long. This is particularly true of Satanism. Larry Zilliox of the Cult Awareness Network makes the point that many adolescents are at a point where they desire some change in their lives, "but they still have to do what others tell them. They think if they worship Satan, he would give them the power to affect change in their lives."

Need for discipline. As virtually every book on child-rearing observes, *kids need limits.* They depend on their parents to show them which behavior is acceptable and what the consequences of bad behavior will be. Many cults are founded on doctrines that spell out in very specific terms exactly what their members must do every minute of every day. Members know what is permitted, what is not, and what the repercussions will be if they fail to toe the line. As Dr. Alexander Deutsch notes, the fact that these rules come from a grandiose religious figure provides the joiner with a powerful kind of substitute parent or conscience. Cult members can thus turn their lives over to this authority figure, who will then show them how to deal with their sexual feelings, their aggressive drives, or their cravings for illicit drugs.

PSYCHIATRIC FACTORS

Elsewhere in this book we made the point not everyone who joins a cult is "crazy." But those people, especially adolescents, who already have a psychiatric condition, or the beginnings of one, are at special risk of falling prey to a cult. Thus *a pre-existing psychological disturbance is one of the most hazardous components in the Formula of Cult Vulnerability.*

One of today's leading authorities on cults, Dr. Marc Galanter, studied members of the Unification Church and the Divine Light Mission. Dr. Galanter and his colleagues found that one out of four members reported having had a serious drug problem before joining the church. Thirty percent had required professional care for mental illness, and 6 percent had been hospitalized. (Other surveys find the percentage of cult members who had previously sought psychotherapeutic treatment to be as high as 60 percent.) Dr. Galanter concluded that people drawn to the church were more likely to have had a psychiatric illness than the general population.

Based on interviews with cult members, Dr. Galanter found that psychological distress in the period prior to joining was an important motivation for becoming involved. Clinicians who worked with these individuals described many of them as "emotionally disturbed, depressed, inadequate, or borderline antisocial youths" or as "lonely, rejected, and sad." Such findings make it clear that some people who join sects do so in order to reduce their sense of personal incompleteness or failure. Some clearly have pre-existent psychopathology; although they join the cult to satisfy their psychopathological needs, their participation leads to adverse emotional effects.

Depression

Recently we treated a young man we'll call Peter. Some months earlier Peter had felt irritable, hopeless, and sad. He believed himself to be the cause of his parents' divorce and thought the world would be better off without him. One day he confided his suicidal thoughts to a friend he had met at school. The next day the friend introduced Peter to members of a group we'll call the Fellowship of Inner Vision. Peter was given a warm welcome and invited to dinner. For the rest of the evening everyone focused on him and his problems. Peter left feeling that there were indeed people who cared about him. Eventually he joined the Fellowship. Six months later he was no longer suicidal, but his growing cult involvement had started to interfere with his personal and scholastic life. He wanted to leave, but felt extremely anxious about doing so and was afraid he would fall back into his previous low mood. That's when he came for help.

Hearing his history, we soon realized that Peter suffered not from "cult-itis" but from depression.

According to Dr. David A. Halperin, cult members usually experience severe depression during the period prior to affiliation. In fact, he sees the act of joining the cult as "an attempt to deal with the intense depression whose source lies in the cult member's difficulty in separating from the original family." Cult membership is a way of forging a more distinct personal identity apart from the family during the transition to adulthood. Recognizing this, many cults refer to themselves as a "family." The leaders often identify themselves as a kind of substitute parent—note that Jim Jones had his followers call him "Dad"; Sun Myung Moon is known more formally as "Father."

Depression—so widespread in our society it is known as the "common cold" of mental disorders—comes in several varieties.

Situational depression is the normal and healthy response to a troubling event such as the death of a loved one, academic pressure, relocation, and so on. Because it stems from a specific problem, situational depression usually lifts when the problem is corrected. Making new friends, improving grades (or dropping out of school), the passage of time—all may help. Aggressive treatment (medications, psychiatric counseling) is not usually needed; perhaps the best remedy is talking with a concerned parent, relative, teacher, friend, or counselor. If your child's depression lasts more than two weeks, though, it may not be situational and you may need to seek outside help.

Major depression is more serious. Some people experience a single episode of major depression; others have recurring bouts. Depression can affect everyone in a different way. Basically, though, the symptoms of adolescent depression are:

- Loss of interest in activities: school, friendships, hobbies, sports
- Change in mood, with significant periods of irritability and anger or sadness and withdrawal
- Sleep disturbance: sleeping more than usual and still feeling tired, or suffering from insomnia.
- Impaired concentration
- Weight change: loss or gain, or continual fluctuation
- Activity level disturbance: alternating periods of agitation or lethargy that change over the course of the day
- Low self-esteem
- Excessive guilt feelings: feeling bad about things that are no one's fault, or taking unnecessary responsibility for a situation
- Suicidal tendencies: preoccupation with death, thoughts of self-injury, or plans for self-punishment. Suicidal acts or threats are a cry for help that *must* be taken seriously

Depression is one form of affective disorder ("affect" means mood). There are others. Manic depression, for example, causes people to experience periods of exhilarating highs and deep lows. Because it results in these swings between two extremes, it is known as bipolar ("two poles") disorder. Another variety is seasonal affective disorder, or SAD. People with SAD experience periods of depression during the winter and return to normal in the spring.

In many cases depression arises from some biological problem—a breakdown in the brain's chemical system responsible for regulating mood. Because it can be biological, depression is often treated very effectively with medications. Psychiatric therapy can also help patients learn how to manage their illness and overcome the damage it has done to their lives.

Conduct Disorder

This term refers to a persistent pattern of disobedience or aggressive behavior toward others. The person with a conduct disorder frequently violates the rights of others or oversteps the rules of society. Teens with conduct disorders lie, cheat, and steal. They may exhibit cruelty to animals and people and show no respect toward the rights and property of others. They start fights, often with weapons; in severe cases, they rape, set fires, break into homes. Between 10 and 15 out of every 100 young people seen in psychiatric clinics are thought to have some form of conduct disorder. Boys with the disorder outnumber girls by over four to one. Because the symptoms overlap, it can sometimes be hard to distinguish a conduct disorder from attention-deficit hyperactivity disorder or a learning disability.

These are some tough customers—physically aggressive, cruel, without concern for the feelings of others, lacking guilt or remorse. Their crimes range from substance abuse, theft, and burglary to rape, arson—even murder at the extreme end of the spectrum. Many of these individuals come from poor families, often without a strong father figure. Their homes are filled with instability, violence, punishment, substance abuse, and threats of abandonment. Sometimes brain damage, learning disabilities, or poor performance in school can trigger symptoms of the disorder.

You can see why some conduct-disordered kids may gravitate toward certain cults, especially Satanic cults, as an "approved" outlet for their destructive impulses. At bottom, their dance with the devil represents nothing more than a way of expressing rebellion and hostility to the outside world.

Attention-deficit Hyperactivity Disorder (ADHD)

Kids with ADHD have no attention span, are impulsive and disorganized, unable to concentrate, and often engage in dangerous activities without considering the consequences. The behavior problems associated with ADHD can disrupt a young person's life.

ADHD, seen in perhaps 3 percent of children, is three to nine times more common in boys than in girls. Typically a child with the disorder does poorly in school and has trouble interacting socially with others. Poor performance or social isolation leads to low self-esteem, changes in mood, low frustration tolerance, and outbursts of temper. Some aspects of the disorder—low concentration, for example—may persist into adulthood. Today's ADHD child is at risk of becoming tomorrow's conduct-disordered adolescent or antisocial adult.

Because they seek thrills and make spontaneous decisions, they may link up with a cult, including Satanism or a quasi-militaristic group, that promises excitement, danger, or power.

Learning Disabilities

Nearly one out of five teenagers has a form of learning disability. Types of disabilities include problems with reading (dyslexia) or writing, difficulty with math or language, and speech impediments. Because learning is painful for these kids, they may be motivated to quit school, making them prone to delinquent behavior or to the appeal of cults.

Adjustment Disorders

Everyone experiences changes, setbacks, or frustrations in life. Such events force us to adapt to new situations. For some people, however, the problem of adjustment persists until it interferes with the ability to function. An adjustment disorder exists when a person has a reaction to a specific life event that impairs the ability to function at school, on the job, or in relationships with others. Such reactions are usually accompanied by either depression or anxiety or both. In 1967 a study found that nearly one out of four college students who dropped out of college because of psychiatric problems were found to have some kind of adjustment disorder. In fact, this diagnosis was the most common, outpacing even depression in frequency.

Adjustment disorder is characterized by a gradual or sudden change in behavior that can be traced to some kind of disruption. The stressor might occur within the family, such as divorce or relocation; it may be related to life developments, such as leaving home for school, taking a job, and so on. Other possible causes include the biological changes of puberty, peer pressure to succeed socially, athletically, or academically; increasing family responsibilities, and so on.

In adolescents, these disorders often derive from the attempts to define oneself; some experts consider all adjustment problems to be a kind of "identity crisis." Persons with the disorder may withdraw from their previous friends or activities, suffer diminished self-esteem, and feel fatigued or depressed. Many young people may feel pressured to establish sexual relationships for which they are unprepared, leading to guilt and anxiety. Others, anxious about leaving home or making "adult" decisions about career and lifestyle before they are really ready, may suddenly reject parents and their values, leading to defiance, conflict, and antisocial behavior. Some join cults.

Substance Abuse

We don't need to document the widespread threats that alcohol and illicit drugs pose to our society. The point we want to make here is simply that the same impulses that lead kids to experiment with drugs can predispose them to flirt with cults as well: social rebellion; the search for thrills or special insight; curiosity; ill-formed faith in mysticism; withdrawal from reality; denial of danger. With their brains under the influence, some cultists come to believe that the "reality" they glimpse while high is also expressed by cult leaders who claim to have had mystic experiences. Ironically, because some cults enforce strict taboos against use of illegal drugs and alcohol, members often stop using these substances and indeed become fierce anti-drug advocates. However some cults (especially Satanic cults) encourage or demand illicit drug consumption, often as part of a ritual.

Schizophrenia

A very small group of cult members—we estimate less than 1 percent—may have some form of schizophrenia. This disorder is characterized by disturbances of language and communication, thought, perception, mood and behavior leading to misinterpretation of reality, delusions, and hallucinations. Some schizophrenic or pre-schizophrenic individuals hear voices. In a few cases kids who hear these voices and can't identify where they came from may start to believe that Satan is speaking directly to them. They may thus be drawn into a Satanic cult, or some other group, or they may merely act as if they are in a cult, in order to deal with the delusion that some supernatural force is ordering them to behave in a certain way. In these rare instances, joining a cult, or acting as if they are in a cult—particularly a Satanic cult—may be the first sign that the individual is schizophrenic.

SOCIAL FACTORS

Socioeconomic Background

While this factor can vary significantly, many cults recruit their members among middle-class whites. For one thing, people in this group may feel a sense of dissatisfaction with their socially approved, mainstream lives. They may be seeking for some kind of unusual experience to lift them out of their daily routine. Also, they may have money at their disposal, money they'd be willing to risk for some kind of elevating experience. Some sociologists observe that streetwise kids who grow up in poor urban neighborhoods develop a kind of radar that alerts them to the presence of hustlers. This radar keeps them from falling prey to a phony line about some cult or other. However, as Joan Ross and Michael Langone point out, some cults— notably Jim Jones' People's Temple— actively recruit among the poor and homeless. And inner-city gangs may serve many of the same functions that cults do: sense of identity, purpose, and so on.

Educational Backgrounds

Having a degree or a diploma doesn't inoculate you from cult influence. On the contrary, some cults are most active on high school and college campuses, seeking to attract kids who feel lonely, isolated, and misunderstood. We'll have more to say about recruitment practices in the next chapter.

Cultural Failure

We've touched on this idea before: Modern society fails to provide many people with adequate ways of interacting with others. Social distance results from several factors, including geographic distance, class distinctions, and the reinforcement of ethnic and cultural identity. A kid who moves to a new city or neighborhood where he is unable to find many social or ethnic peers may latch on to a cult in order to feel he belongs.

Peer Pressure and Media Pressure

In our culture ideas and fads are spread through mass media. The pressure on kids to adopt the behavior they see on TV and in the movies, and to embrace attitudes they hear blaring through their radios and boom boxes, is enormous. In order to belong, to be accepted by their peers, kids will strive to conform, even if they risk their health or sanity in doing so.

Much of the substance abuse, sexual acting out, and the cult behavior we see today can be traced directly to the pressure from the mass media. As Dr. Henry Work notes, "These pressures take advantage of the normal phenomena of growth during this period: the search for independence, identity, and conformity with the peer group. Equally, every psychological discovery of the scientific world has been utilized by societal forces trying to influence the activities, behavior, and lifestyles" of the youth in this country. For some kids, cults satisfy their needs to belong or to rebel.

THE FAMILY FACTOR

How significant is the family in our Formula of Vulnerability? Does coming from a broken home, or from a background where religion is highly emphasized, inevitably propel a youngster toward a cult?

As we saw earlier, such is not necessarily the case. A number of solid scientific studies have shown that family traits and interactions are *not* a major aspect of cult susceptibility.

One study, for example, set out to determine whether the families of cult members were overinvested emotionally in their children and demonstrated a lack of flexibility in problem-solving. Results showed that enmeshment and rigidity are no more a universal trait of cult-involved families, or of individual family members, than in any other "normal" family. And in Dr. Neil Maron's study cited earlier, none of the predicted traits—psychopathology, moral emphasis, and so on—proved to have any bearing on whether or not the adolescent joined a cult.

This is not to say that family dynamics are completely irrelevant. Some studies have found a possible connection between cult membership and the degree of criticism and emotional expression among family members. Our experience convinces us, and surveys confirm the fact, that a teen's decision to join a cult is often made at a stressful time: during a crisis, an important transition, or after a significant loss. Some of these stresses are directly related to family life—for example, a parent's illness or death, loss of income, or failure of a business. In many instances youngsters leave home for the first time when they head off for college; yet some families haven't done all they could to prepare their sons and daughters for this new overwhelming sense of independence and responsibility. Cults know this, and work hard to lure kids who feel lonely, afraid, and cut off from their home base.

Families today face an uphill struggle to stay intact. Financial pressure, the demands of child-rearing, the unrelenting search for personal satisfaction—any of these factors alone can cause a family to disintegrate. As Dr. Louis West notes, "Vulnerability to cults is not the only consequence of this disintegration. Increases in violence, drug abuse, crime, and delinquency all relate to serious problems in families." He adds: "While it does not appear to me that family problems are significantly more frequent in the backgrounds of cult recruits than in other persons with the same demographic characteristics, it is also true that interventions involving families have often proved helpful in solving cult-related problems." In other words, family problems may not lead to cult membership, but helping families resolve their difficulties can help draw the adolescent back into the family fold.

Why do kids join cults? As we've seen, the answer depends on the mix of individual, psychological, and social factors. One child may be motivated to sign on because of the clash between the sexual and emotional changes of puberty and a growing sense of social isolation. Intellectual curiosity might mix with incipient depression to drive another youngster into the hands of a therapeutically oriented group. Given the right circumstances, any combination of variables can lead to cult involvement. Cults use subtle and devious means to identify and exploit a teen's weak spots, as we'll see in the next chapter.

5

HOW CULTS PREY ON KIDS

The leaders of most organized cults and their handpicked, carefully trained lieutenants usually know how to identify a person's weak spots and exploit those weaknesses for their own ends. Like chameleons, they can change their skins as needed to blend in with their background. Only when they are sure of their grip on their victim do they reveal their true colors.

In the previous chapter we described the factors that contribute to an individual's cult susceptibility. Now let's look at the techniques cults use to lure potential members and convert them to a new—and possibly dangerous—way of thinking. Please bear in mind that some less organized cults, especially Satanic cults, may not use these techniques.

MEETING THE NEED

Maria fought back tears as she told the story of her son's involvement with a destructive cult. "They must have drugged him and kidnapped him," she said in a choked voice. "Len would never fall for such a scam. He's too smart for that. They've brainwashed him—I know they have. It's the only way they could have made him turn against his family."

This distraught mother was fighting the idea that her son might have chosen to join a cult *voluntarily*. She had trouble accepting the possibility that Len was looking for something he couldn't get from his relationships with family or friends. Understandably upset, she accused the cult of stealing her son through coercion, drugs, and brainwashing—anything to avoid facing the thought that Len had acted under his own volition.

Group affiliation has very real appeal. Joining a group provides a sense of identity, community, and commitment. Churches, civic organizations, and clubs can fulfill those needs. So can cults. In most cases, cults don't need to bash recruits over the head and drag them off. The innate desire to belong is often all it takes to get the ball rolling. Much of the rest is nothing more than marketing.

The Need for Identity

We define ourselves in large measure through our relationships with others. Identity, in one sense of the word, means the characteristics by which someone is recognized as a member of a group. Adolescence is a time when much of our identity is forged. Associating with a group lets us feel special and develop a sense of self-worth.

There are other benefits as well. People under stress seek out others who have suffered similar experiences. They exchange notes and learn to put their problems in some kind of perspective. Knowing that others can identify with them— that someone else has "been there too"—assures them that they are not alone or abnormal and reduces their fear and anxiety.

Normally such associations are beneficial. But there could be some danger as well. People who find themselves in strange or unfamiliar situations—certain group meetings, for example— experience emotional turmoil. The nervous system reacts, adrenaline flows, and emotions heighten. Research shows that in such a setting, people tend to interpret their feelings according to what other people tell them. For example, visitors at a revival meeting who get caught up in the jubilation of the event might experience a new sense of elation or warmth. If they express those feelings to another person, they may be told something like, "That's the spirit working inside you, brother!" Interpreting feelings for someone else in this way usually poses no problem if the group is benign.

The trouble comes when cynical charismatic leaders exploit this human tendency to interpret their emotions based on cues from other people. Such leaders will stage encounters or events for the sole purpose of stirring up new or troubling emotions in the participants. These leaders, or their carefully trained minions, then interpret those feelings as "the work of the Devil" or "proof that you need to sign up for our series of Insight Workshops" or whatever the going racket is.

The Need for Community

Groups can offer their members many valuable benefits: closeness with like-minded individuals, acceptance, love, an attitude of caring and support, and the chance to act in positive ways to make a difference in the world. Membership is usually a two-way street; an individual benefits by helping someone else and by being helped in turn.

As we have seen, humans are biologically as well as socially adapted to band together in groups. Cults depend on this basic fact of evolution. Dr. Saul Levine notes, "The sense of belonging cannot be overemphasized" in considering how cults function.

In their recruiting drives, cults exploit the need for community in several ways. First, of course, they offer an opportunity for group involvement. But what's more, they deliberately seek out people who may be isolated, who feel cut off from society. Young college students fill the bill quite nicely. Many of them are away from home for the first time, isolated from old friends and family. They may not have had time to make new associations. They have left their teen-age lives behind but have not yet crossed the line into adulthood. Lastly, many cults attract members not because their philosophy is so appealing but because they stress a sense of comradery. In fact, many cults operate in disguise; they don't even discuss their particular dogma, let alone reveal it, until weeks after the recruit has shown some interest in the group.

The Need for Exclusivity

Although we humans need groups, we need those groups to be of manageable size. It doesn't seem to satisfy our need to associate simply to say we belong to the Race of Humankind. No, we are compelled to draw more lines around ourselves, to make further divisions between "us" and "them." Such divisions may be ethnic, cultural, religious, racial, philosophical—or all of the above simultaneously.

Ironically, though, no matter how small the group, there seems to be a tendency to break into even smaller units. Some cults—the Hare Krishnas and the Rajneeshees, for example—have attracted members to several communes throughout the world. Although supposedly united by a common philosophy, members tend to form attitudes and relationships unique to their specific location. As Dr. Levine points out, these smaller groups, and not the larger movement, become the top priority for the members. Another danger to add to the list, then, is that a cult may start off with benign intent, but a local branch of that cult may develop an identity of its own and lose sight of its founders' goals.

The Need for Relief of Emotional Distress

Earlier we saw that, according to a study by cult authority Marc Galanter, three out of ten Unification Church members had sought professional help for emotional problems prior to joining the cult. The same study found that nearly 40 percent of Divine Light Mission members had received treatment, and that 9 percent had been hospitalized. Such findings support the idea that many people enter cults during a time of emotional turmoil, and that one reason for joining is to reduce their level of anxiety and anguish.

Some cult leaders seem to have a kind of psychic radar that senses what's troubling a potential recruit. Or they extract highly personal information from the recruit through such techniques as confrontational group meetings or forced confessions. The leaders then portray their cult as the only way to solve the problem. Cults thus stir up a member's sense of guilt or fear while at the same time offering to relieve these troubling feelings. The horrors committed during a Satanic ritual—often combined with substance abuse—can also cause guilt and help to bond the teen to the cult.

The Need for Commitment and Discipline

Without commitment no goal can be set; without discipline no goal can be reached. (In this context "discipline" does not mean punishment; it means the self-control needed to achieve a desired goal.)

But some young people today are brought up in an atmosphere of permissiveness and freedom. Their parents are fearful of setting too many limits or restraining their creative impulses. By the same token, they don't encourage their children to set goals for themselves and to know the satisfaction of achieving those goals. As a result, their children flail about, and parents assume or rationalize that settling down will occur with time. Some of these attitudes are fallout from the 1960s, when "doing your own thing" was the order of the day. However, for many parents these permissive attitudes are really apologies for their parental failures. A child today faces difficult circumstances: single-parent homes, where parental supervision may be minimal, tension-filled homes where the argumentative parents cannot financially afford to separate, prosperous homes where two working parents are emotionally unavailable to their children.

Kids need guidance. They need boundaries. Of course, they may perceive boundaries simply as restrictions on their freedom and go into a rage whenever anyone sets limits for them. Some are drawn to Satanism, for example, as a way of expressing their rebellion against discipline. But our experience in working with adolescents convinces us that, deep down, most kids are usually glad to know that someone is keeping an eye on them, preventing them from going too far over the edge. They may know the risks of burning out on drugs or the dangers of sexual freedom, including disease and pregnancy, but may be unable to control their behavior. A guiding hand at the right moment can prevent disaster.

If parents or other authority figures won't supply discipline, then some kids will look for it on their own. They may be drawn to sports or martial arts, or may even respond to the challenge of figuring out the latest video game. Of course, some will be drawn to cults, relying on the leader to lay down the ground rules for proper behavior. In addition, some cults, especially Satanic ones, encourage wild behavior—"if it feels good, do it."

The Need for Leadership

None of us knows every answer or has had every possible experience. We all turn to others at some time to help fill in the blanks in our lives, to show us the way or help us if we stumble. There is much to be gained from submitting to the benevolent authority or teacher who offers guidance, strength, security, and solutions.

Sadly, however, many cult leaders are cynical victimizers who take advantage of naive and credulous people to further their own ends. Most cults are set up so that there is a single, totalitarian leader at the head. These leaders often claim they have had some magical, mystical experience that gave them special powers. People who are attracted to cults seem more than willing to attribute such remarkable characteristics to their leaders, perhaps as a way of justifying their own involvement.

In order to make their vision come to pass, cult leaders must manipulate others into doing their bidding. They thus exercise total control over every aspect of members' lives. Ironically, founders of cults may be less despotic than their lieutenants, who struggle to outdo each other in enforcing the cult's dogmatic principles in order to gain the guru's favor. As Dr. Levine puts it, those on the rung below the leader are the epitome of true believers—unwavering, inflexible, even intolerant.

RECRUITING TECHNIQUES

How does a cult "advertise" itself? How does it apply enough pressure to potential recruits to get them to join without scaring them off? From what we've seen, some of their strategies—combining affection with deception—would impress the most seasoned Madison Avenue ad exec.

Some cults do it directly, putting up notices in grocery stores, community centers, and school bulletin boards. Others use their vast economic power to organize recruitment drives. Many cults have grown so large that they are more like corporations than religious movements. Sun Myung Moon owns dozens of businesses, ranging from commercial fisheries to newspapers. The Hare Krishnas recently created a huge religious retreat and tourist center in West Virginia. Transcendental Meditation markets its techniques as a leisure-time activity.

Scientology markets itself aggressively, taking out ads in the Yellow Pages and promoting *Dianetics* books through extensive TV advertising. Members even put up billboards depicting a raging volcano and urging readers to "clear" themselves of their problems.

For one-on-one contact, clean-cut, good-looking young Scientologists scout for possible recruits at college functions or on the street and invite them to a "party." The party often turns out to be a chance for Scientologists to use a device called an "E-meter." Subjects are hooked up to these modified lie detectors and asked to describe intimate details of their past. The "E-meter" then supposedly identifies the recruit's "engrams"—imprints on the cells of the body caused by traumatic or stressful events. By identifying and reliving these events (through a prolonged series of expensive instructional classes), a person supposedly eliminates the engrams and thus eliminates inner turmoil. Going even further, Scientologists tell members that they also have to clear the engrams from all of their *past* lives as well. Hubbard claimed his therapeutic techniques could cure illness, restore eyesight to the blind, and improve intelligence and appearance. The FDA, we should add, has a somewhat lower opinion of the E-meter's therapeutic value.

Other cults are less subtle. The Hare Krishnas, for example, stand out in a crowd: The heads of the men are shaved, except for a pony tail at the back, and they may have paint on their foreheads. They wear saffron-colored robes, while the women wear traditional Indian garments. Members of the group visit college campuses, bus terminals, and airports, singing and accompanying themselves with portable organs, drums, and finger cymbals. They share their sweet vegetarian meals with passersby, sell copies of their magazine *Back to Godhead*, and invite people to visit their local temple. Conversely, Satanic cults are very secretive.

As we've discussed, colleges are an important locus for recruiting activities. One more point about that: Parents often live out their own fantasies through their child. They want their son or daughter to have opportunities they never knew, to attend schools they could never afford. If they aren't careful, they may blind themselves to their child's own special needs and interests, and steer their youngster toward a competitive, impersonal university that offers little of the support the child wants or needs. Dr. David Halperin points out that in such circumstances, cults may appear to supply the missing support and promise the kid a simpler world based on faith. In so doing they play on his resentment toward the family who banished him to the school that is now causing him so much anxiety.

Some cults spread their message through the modern miracle of desktop publishing. Anybody with access to a xerox machine can manufacture copies of a cult's holy books. Many of these find their way to small bookshops devoted to the New

Age or other eccentric philosophies. Satanic bibles and books on witchcraft are easily found on the shelves of the country's many occult bookshops.

A common method of proselytizing is to create some event that attracts altruistic, idealistic young people. One group, for example, sets up peace marches for high school students, then, seizing on the momentum, encourages participants to stay involved in the pease effort by joining the cult. Other groups might sponsor "discussion groups" or portray themselves as volunteer help organizations.

Sadly, this ploy—misleading people about the nature of the group—is very widespread. Many cults use false names or create "front" organizations to disguise their true origins. One cult refers to its practices as "heavenly deception."

Why? If the cult thinks it has something of value to offer, why should it be scared to show its face?

Richard Delgado, an expert in the legal aspects of cults, states: "When a newcomer attends his or her first [cult] meeting or training session, ordinarily the capacity to make a free, rational choice is unimpaired. The young person may be experiencing some rather ordinary life crisis (leaving home, attending college, breaking up with a boyfriend or girlfriend), but his or her faculties are generally intact. If, in this condition, the individual were confronted with the full truth about the organization—its name, leader, the demands it will later place on members—he or she would respond by leaving. Consequently, many groups conceal these items of information until the group perceives the recruit is 'ready' for them."

The use of this strategy reflects the group's own awareness of the bad publicity cults have received, especially during the 1970s, when horror stories of cults and deprogramming were common. Naturally, these cults understand that so much negative exposure would cause people to avoid having anything to do with the cult.

But there's a deeper, more insidious reason. Cult leaders

know that what draws members is not necessarily the group's philosophy. The attraction, as we've discussed, has more to do with a person's search for friendship and association, and the need to discover a focus to one's life. The nuts and bolts of the ideology—the talk about "engrams" or "Krishna"—is almost irrelevant. It behooves the cult to get recruits involved *first*, and then reveal the cult's beliefs. The Unification Church learned this lesson over 20 years ago. In the late 1960s the group held a number of public lectures in which speakers outlined the tenets of their religion. Only a few people came, and even fewer joined. As Dr. Brant Wenegrat notes, the Church only succeeded in boosting its membership when it put ideology on the back burner and changed its recruiting methods.

The primary Unification Church recruiting technique is known by the somewhat chilling name of "love-bombing." Barbara Underwood, a former member, defines "love-bombing" as a "persistent psychological effort to disarm a skeptical recruit by excessive attention in order to get him or her into the cult." Potential new members are invited to the cult's commune for dinner or some other social meeting at which they are fed and given lots of emotional strokes. Members bend over backwards to make the new people feel special, important, and needed. Other groups soften up recruits through such methods as chanting, sleep deprivation, peer pressure, even hostile confrontation designed to shake them out of their complacency.

If the recruit shows a glimmer of interest, he or she may be invited to a longer, more intensive "retreat" or some other such event. Not until then, or even later, is the group's purpose and philosophy revealed. Usually at that point recruits have been so softened up that they are unable to resist the pressure to join the group. At that point, adopting the cult's dogma is not a question of undergoing some kind of wrenching conversion. It is instead simply a matter of embracing the reality of the recruit's new social group—or, as sociologists J. Lofland and R. Stark put it, "to accept the opinions of one's friends."

SUFFER THE CHILDREN

Our focus in this chapter is on the ways cults prey on young people. For the most part we are referring to subtle ways cults lure their victims and inculcate their ideas. But there's an even uglier side to the story: the way cults abuse children, physically as well as psychologically.

In recent years news reports have told about day-care centers where children were forced to play sick games and act out sexual behavior. Other stories tell about children kidnapped and murdered as part of cult rituals. Skeptics claim that such reports are wildly exaggerated, that children—unreliable witnesses known for their overactive imaginations—are making the whole thing up or misinterpreting what they have seen.

As parents, you have no doubt been troubled by such reports. You probably have asked yourselves, what is really going on?

Sad to say, we feel that such reports of cult abuse must be taken seriously. Not all the reports turn out to be true, but those that are true violate our sense of humanity and civilization.

Satanism, for example, operates by turning Christianity on its head. Because Christians hold that children are special to God, Satanic cults believe that hurting children represents a victory in the battle to rule the universe. In our clipping file are many stories of children being stolen and used for human sacrifices, particularly during the Satanic "holidays." Sometimes cult members desecrate graveyards, digging up a child's coffin to use the skull and bones in its rites. Some law enforcement officers dismiss grave-robbing as a teenage prank, and some of it may be just that. But such "pranks" may also indicate that someone has gone from being a dabbler in Satanism to being a full-fledged practitioner.

Other cults abuse children in a number of ways. Space doesn't permit a full description of all the possibilities. Briefly, though, some cults look on children not as individuals but as "possessions," as clay to be molded after the cult's view of the world. Some cults, like the People's Temple, break up families and separate parents from their children to indoctrinate them with the group's philosophy. A group in Canada labels children born outside the cult as "bastards"; those born within the cult are "Christ Children." The cult leader breeds with selected female members of the sect to produce offspring he calls the "New Root Race."

Documented evidence shows that some cults inflict physical abuse on children, including beatings, torture, incest, starvation, sexual abuse, and denial of food or medical care. Forms of psychological abuse may include isolation, emotional manipulation, withholding of nurture and care, and mind control. Sometimes the child is punished by the leader of by all the members; sometimes the punishment is meted out by his own parents.

Obviously, if you are reading this book, you are concerned about how to prevent your child's involvement with a cult, or how to bring such involvement to an end. You should be aware, however, that a new generation of cult members is springing up. This generation is made up of children born to *parents* who have been involved with cults for years. Such families do not necessarily live in a cult commune. They may live anywhere and lead basically normal lives. However, they may keep their children out of school, or deny them regular medical care in the belief that "God will cure them if they have love in their heart."

Of all cult practices, perhaps none is more cruel or more evil than the brutalization of an innocent child.

BECOMING—AND STAYING—A MEMBER

Anyone who has tried to convert from one mainstream religion to another knows that doing so is none too easy. Most religions play devil's advocate, putting up hurdles that potential converts must overcome as tests of their devotion and understanding. Nor do religions solicit new members primarily among people who are weak, depressed, and vulnerable.

But *anyone* can join a cult. Just sign here.

Once recruits become pledges, they experience a flood of new feelings. Their sense of alienation, loneliness, and self-hatred is swept away, replaced by self-righteousness and a renewed sense of self-esteem. They are on an emotional high, having rediscovered a sense of purpose and meaning in their lives. Understandably they want to share their elation with others and are eager to talk to outsiders, usually in an effort to convince them to join the movement, too. Some cult leaders capitalize on this impulse by sending new members out to proselytize among the unconverted or to spend grueling hours panhandling for change. The cult thus continues to operate because these eager new members are blind to the fact that they are being exploited. If a member has an inkling that something may be wrong, the cult squelches the notion, stressing that uncertainty or guilt are the workings of Satan or some other dark force.

One key to success is isolation. Cults must separate their members from family and other outside forces who might try to lure them away. This explains why so many cults structure themselves as surrogate families, complete with "Dads" and "Moms" at their head. "Moonies," for example, are taught to consider Reverend Moon and his wife as their "True Parents." The Sullivanians have been accused of preaching that the nuclear family is evil, and insisting that members have almost no contact with parents except to ask for money.

Isolation, then, is a form of control, not just over body but over mind. Cults perpetuate themselves and tighten their grip on members through an astonishing range of mind-control techniques. Some people call this brainwashing. But such a term isn't really adequate, since it implies that members are simply passive victims of indoctrination. As we have seen, many people who join cults are actively searching for answers and become willing partners in the process of turning off thought processes and shutting out the rest of the world. A list of common mind-control methods appears in the Box on page 67.

Cult Indoctrination and Mind-Control Techniques*

- Subtle process of introduction of the convert and his gradual discovery of the real hosts
- Overpowering techniques: love-bombing, offering a free meal at an international center for friends, flirting, "fishing" techniques (prostitution as a method of recruitment)
- Ready-made answers and decisions forced upon recruits
- Flattery
- Distributing money or medicine
- Requiring unconditional surrender to the cult leader
- Isolation: control of the rational thinking process, elimination of outside information and influence (family, friends, newspapers, magazines, television, radio, medical treatment, and so forth)
- Removing recruits from their past lives; focusing on past deviant behavior such as drug use, sexual misdeeds, playing on psychological hangups, poor social relationships, and so on
- Consciousness-altering methods leading to disturbed thoughts (intellectual bombardment); use of thought-stopping clichés; closed system of logic; restricting reflective thinking
- Keeping recruits constantly busy and never alone; continually exhorting and training in order to arrive at an exalted spiritual status, altered consciousness, and automatic submission to directives; stifling resistance and negativity; responding to the member's fear so that even greater fear is aroused
- Strong focus on the leader

---

* Adapted from a report of the Vatican conference "Sects or New Religious Movements," Rome, May 3, 1986 and cited in *Cults and New Religious Movements*, M. Galanter, ed. Washington DC: American Psychiatric Association, 1989.

Remember, too, the point we made earlier: people placed in a highly charged emotional situation are inclined to believe it is a positive experience simply because other people *tell* them so. Often cult life leads to a mystical or transcendental event—seeing a vision of heaven, or being overwhelmed by an intense bright light. Such experiences, Dr. Galanter points out, are crucial for conversion to the cult and for encouraging continued participation among members. A brother member might say, for example: "You saw the Light? Fabulous—that proves you are meant to be with us!"

Of course, not everyone *is* meant to be in a cult. Some who blunder their way into a group's clutches might want to get out, but are physically and emotionally powerless to do so. In the next chapter we'll talk about some of the options available for rescuing cult victims, and ways of helping them following their return to reality.

6

Breaking the Spell: Leaving the Cult

When a teen joins a cult, the impact on a family can be shattering. Parents may fear—and with good reason—that their son or daughter might be physically or psychologically harmed. They may be worried—again with good reason—that they will be prevented from seeing their child or having any further contact. On another level, they may feel resentful if the child seems to have discarded his real mother and father and has taken up with a surrogate family. Parents may perceive the child as rejecting the family's values and traditions—everything the family believes in and stands for. The parents may have worked hard and sacrificed much to prepare a path for their child. By suddenly shifting directions, the child can shatter their dreams—and break their hearts.

The reactions parents have on hearing about their child's cult involvement cover a spectrum. At one extreme are those parents who calmly accept the situation and who may do nothing to change it. At the other end are those who, shocked and alarmed, try to move heaven and earth to rescue their child. In the middle are parents who feel torn and ambivalent, uncertain what to do, or whether to do anything at all. The most common response, however, is anger and a sense of urgency.

Before we go much further, we should point out that most people who join cults decide to leave them voluntarily within two years. Many Satanic dabblers, for instance, lose interest in the occult when they realize how much discipline and effort such practices require. Although perhaps one out of three ex-cultists show some evidence of psychological disturbance following their departure, some will emerge none the worse for wear. Dr. Saul Levine notes that, in many cases, the process of leaving a cult is an intense life experience which winds up contributing in important ways to an individual's growth and development.

The problem of "rescuing" someone from a cult is a knotty one, tangles as it is by issues of religious expression, tolerance, freedom of speech, and personal autonomy. There are legal, moral, and philosophical issues to consider. Fortunately, as we'll see in this chapter, there are several options available to parents who need help, options that range from self-help groups and support networks to professional guidance. We'll also describe the role psychiatrists may play, as they may be able to do a great deal of good in these trying circumstances. As Drs. Paul Hamburg and David Hoffman have stated, psychiatrists "are trained to comprehend complex clinical situations with several layers of meaning, and know how to relieve suffering in situations where a cure is not immediately at hand." They add that, through commitment to passionate open inquiry, "the psychiatrist is in an ideal position to help a cult member and his or her family understand the complex dilemmas of cult affiliation." And a psychiatrist can treat any underlying psychiatric conditions.

PREVENTION

We realize that this may seem obvious, but the easiest way to handle the problem of cult involvement is to prevent it from occurring in the first place.

Prevention is largely a product of education. Teaching children about cults alerts them, first, to their existence and, second, to the tricks they pull to attract new members. The best setting for this education is the home. As parents, you are doing your part by reading this book and becoming alert to the warning signs of cult involvement. We urge you to continue your efforts: be aware of cult-related news items; check your library for books and other sources of information. Most important, discuss what you have learned with others in your family and your community. It's easier to address the problem *before* it strikes, when everyone is calm, than to try to put out the fire once it starts.

Schools and civic groups can help by sponsoring classes or seminars on cults and their methods. We talk about sex and drugs in such settings; surely we can find a way to discuss another life-threatening problem facing today's youth. As a parent, you might be able to get the ball rolling by speaking with your local principal or parent-teacher group, or by contacting one of the parent support networks for help in doing so (see Appendix). We should note, too, that many cults have already established a foothold on high school and college campuses. They register as "official" student groups and thus are given license to use school facilities to form clubs, hold meetings, run seminars, and so on. By alerting school officials to this tactic, you might subvert expansion of the cult.

One other point: As we have seen, adolescents often experience deep feelings of depression as they attempt to separate from their families and develop new, independent identities. Do all you can to help your youngster during this difficult and troubling time. Encourage his efforts to break free, foster his independence—but let him know he can always count on you for support. Love may not be all you need, but it surely helps.

VOLUNTARY DEPARTURE

Remember that many cult members pull out under their own steam within a year or two. Of course, the longer they stay, the harder it is for them to quit, and the more disturbed they may be once free.

Many factors can lead to the choice to quit. Some former members report that they became disappointed in one or more aspects of cult life. They may simply dislike communal living, or they may resent the fact that they live in poverty while the cult's leaders revel in luxury. They may be literally sick and tired of panhandling all day and attending classes and lectures all evening. Or they may sense problems in the basic tenets of the group's philosophy, feeling that the group is moving away from the principles that attracted the member in the first place. In some cases they have moved up the ladder of the organization, and have been given access to—and put off by—some of the cult's more esoteric "secrets." One former member of a cult, for example, told us she was appalled when she heard the details of the cult's cosmic vision, a scenario that involves reincarnation, galactic confederations, and a 75-million-year-old alien named Xenu. "This isn't religion," she said, "it's a bad *Star Trek* episode."

Other people leave because they get hurt. Cults can brutalize their members, mentally and physically. Punishments may range from beatings to being locked in cages or airless rooms. Jim Jones castigated some of his followers by forcing them to masturbate or to have intercourse with people they detested in front of the entire camp, including the children. People with relatively strong personalities are more able to override the cult's influence over them and break away. Sometimes, though, the attempt to leave may be fraught with peril. In the case of the People's Temple, the defection of four followers caused "Dad" to believe that the end had come and triggered the notorious mass suicide.

One of the most important things you can do to encourage your child to leave a cult voluntarily is to *stay in touch*. Let her realize you still care, that you will leave the door open and a light burning in the window. She may not be consciously aware of it, but she will keep it in the back of her mind that her family offers a possible path of escape should she begin to question the wisdom of staying with the cult.

INVOLUNTARY DEPARTURE ("DEPROGRAMMING")

Barbara Underwood, a former "Moonie" who went through a wrenching process of extrication from the cult, wrote of her experience in a book called *Hostage to Heaven*. As she puts it:

> I joined the Unification Church because I thought I'd found the ultimate truth. I left the cult because I realized during the course of my deprogramming—in an environment where I was free for the first time in four years to reflect, question, and examine—that the truth wasn't black and white. I discovered it wasn't that my own faith in God was inauthentic; I'd wrongly worshipped a "God" that Moon's Principles had created in my mind, a "God" who mistrusted individual freedom of will. . . . [The deprogramming] allowed me to be an individual, not a cultist, and . . . to discover that in the cult I hadn't owned or had access to a private inner life of truth, free of guilt or manipulation.

During the 1970s especially, deprogramming made headlines. In print and on the air, people told of being kidnapped, hustled into cars, locked in motel rooms, and subjected to days of intensive instruction. In some cases, the deprogramming failed; the member, having been terrorized, returned to the cult. Others, like Barbara Underwood, remembered it as "a compassionate experience with loving and well-informed people."

Father William Kent Burtner, a Dominican priest who counsels former cult victims, defines deprogramming as "a counseling process whereby a cult victim is given the opportunity to see a broad perspective on his/her group; to see more fully the implications of membership; to learn the rudiments of abusive behavior modification techniques and thought reform processes; to examine the values, tenets, and practices of the group; to examine his/her own thoughts and feelings so that the person reevaluates the affiliation and makes a free personal choice." Ted Patrick, perhaps the most well-known deprogrammer, describes the process as a way of "jump-starting" the mind to get it working again.

Deprogramming has some advantages. It removes the member from the cult's sphere of influence and creates a 24-hour-a-day environment in which the member can reevaluate his situation. It can be a relatively short process—a few days or a week—although the transition period that follows may last much longer. Often the entire process is handled by a team of experienced deprogrammers, including former cult members. In extreme cases it may be the only option open to the family. Studies show that deprogramming is much more likely to succeed if the member has been with the cult less than a year.

There are drawbacks, though. The process is expensive, costing perhaps $10,000 or more. You don't just find "deprogrammers" in the Yellow Pages, nor is there any kind of licensed training procedure for those who do the actual work. Because it is coercive, it involves secrecy and deceit, which may add to the family's stress, or if it involves an adult, it may technically be considered kidnapping. Nor is deprogramming guaranteed. Although about 70 percent of people who are deprogrammed stay out of the cult, the rest, feeling an even deeper loyalty, return to the fold where they are given a hero's welcome. Cults have been known to sue or otherwise harass families who tried to deprogram members. Besides, as we have seen, many cult members would eventually leave the group voluntarily anyway. And in some cases the parents are so focused on extricating their children that they make no provision to meet their many psychological needs during the long period of post-cult adjustment.

Deprogramming is a controversial technique. As we said, it doesn't always work. And it raises legal questions about civil rights, freedom of religion, and freedom of speech. In the last decade, as more research has been done on the effects of cult religious movements, the trend has shifted away from coercive deprogramming and toward what is now known as "exit counseling." This shift resulted partly from the growing involvement of psychiatrists, psychologists, and social workers in helping families and individuals deal with cult-related problems. Some of those problems include depression, guilt, loneliness, indecisiveness, poor judgment, simplistic thinking, fear of retribution, difficulty communicating, problems with family relationships, and the existence of a spiritual void in the ex-member's life. As we'll see, psychiatric treatment can help relieve many of these post-cult symptoms.

LEGAL RECOURSE

We don't have space here to outline all the legal avenues available to you. Each state has different laws concerning cult activity and the rights of the family. In passing, though, you should know that some people have successfully worked with the judicial system in their efforts to rescue their loved ones from the clutches of a cult. Sometimes parents have their cult-involved child declared incapable of managing her own affairs; this empowers them to hold the child against her will. Some lawsuits are motivated by the parents' desire to protect their own property or to keep children from signing their inheritance over to the cult. Contact your lawyer or the cult support network for more information.

PSYCHIATRIC HELP

Throughout this book we've emphasized the fact that cult involvement is in many ways a family issue. Cults attract adolescents who stand on the cusp of adulthood—still largely dependent on their parents and plagued with ambivalence about leaving the family to strike out on their own. Joining a cult often symbolizes rejection of the family and all it stands for. The responsibility for rescuing the cult member lies almost exclusively with the family; the chances of success depend on the strength of the ties between parents and children, and between husband and wife as well. For those reasons, the psychiatric approach to managing cult-related problems works best when it focuses not just on the individual member but on the entire family.

If you decide to seek professional help, you should be aware that the exact role a psychiatrist plays in the process depends on several factors. Therapy for people who have been involved with the cult for only a short time is different than in cases of long-term involvement. And a member who has actually left the cult will need a different approach entirely. The doctor also needs to determine whether some kind of underlying emotional or personality disorder is involved in order to treat such a problem correctly. With increasing frequency, some parents ask the psychiatrist to become involved for legal, rather than medical, reasons—for example, to testify to the dangers of cults or to the psychic damage caused by "brainwashing."

What qualifications should you look for in a psychiatrist? To begin with, any caregiver you deal with should communicate a sense of compassion for your situation. He or she should be trained to handle the special needs and problems of adolescents, and should also demonstrate a solid understanding of cult-related issues. Not all professionals feel comfortable dealing with cases involving group psychology (or psychopathology), or involving such profound moral and religious—not to mention legal—questions. Don't hesitate to ask for evidence of expertise in this field. You won't have the best shot at success unless you do.

It's unlikely that an adolescent will walk into a doctor's office on his own and ask for help. Normally the parents call for an appointment. In many cases they wait until their child's behavior has gotten out of control, when a crisis exists. Whatever the situation, the first step is for the family to come in for an evaluation. Of course, it's much better if the cult member can be present, but that's not always possible.

The psychiatrist's goal in these initial consultations is to clarify exactly what is happening. The questions we ask are designed to reveal how everyone feels about the situation in general and about the cult member in particular. It's important to get a picture of the cult member's personality, his strengths and weaknesses. We also want to determine the extent to which the feelings that other people in the family have about the cult member are the product of their own ambivalent attitudes. This is especially important if the cult member is not there to speak for himself. One result of such questioning may be a redefinition of the situation. In some cases, for example, it seems that the problem is not so much cult membership or a mental disorder, but an absence of healthy discipline in the child's life.

Sometimes the result of these first sessions is that the family clears up some of their differences and organizes into a united front. Now able to concentrate on the problem at hand, they mobilize themselves for action. If they have followed the psychiatrist's advice and kept the lines of contact open and nonchallenging, they may inspire the cult member to reconsider his affiliation. This is more likely to happen if the child has been involved with the cult for only a short time. In a few cases it turns out that there is no real problem. If a child who announces his interest in a cult is functioning well otherwise— handling his schoolwork, exhibiting no negative changes in behavior, able to maintain good relationships with friends—the issue may have more to do with parental intolerance than cult influence.

As we have seen, cult membership involves a combination of religious, social, emotional, and psychological factors. The process of evaluating the situation requires sensitive questioning on the part of the caregiver. A psychiatrist will consider the problem from many different angles. For example, is there a *medical* problem that can be identified and treated? Does the child have a major affective disorder or a psychosis of some kind? What medical or laboratory tests might provide important clues? If a biomedical problem exists, what treatments will help—psychotherapy, medications, hospitalization? What *psychological* issues are involved—personal relationships, significant losses, developmental problems? Which psychological tests will help fill in some of the details of the situation? And how healthy is the *family*? Might some problem between the parents have triggered the movement toward the cult? Does the problem lie, not with the child, but with the mother or father, or with all parties?

If you seek professional help, you will be asked to supply a great deal of information about yourself, your child, and your family. The doctor will need to learn about your religious background and practices as well as your child's reasons for joining and staying with the cult. Other questions may focus on your child's personality before joining the cult—mental health, state of mind, experiences in school and at work, relationships with friends and relatives. Is the child sexually active? Does he use alcohol or illicit drugs? What changes have you noticed since he joined the cult? Don't be surprised if your doctor asks you to supply information about the specific cult involved: philosophy, the nature of its leadership, rituals and practices. With hundreds of cults in existence, it's not possible to keep up-to-date on every one of them. Remember, you are working together with your doctor as a team to help your child.

During this phase your psychiatrist will work to support you and your efforts to deal with the problem, recognizing that you are motivated by concern, not over whether your child has adopted some strange religion, but whether he is in some kind of danger. At all times the emphasis should be on the need to maintain contact with your child and keep the lines of communication open. You can't make progress if you are defensive or judgmental. Such attitudes will only drive a wedge between you and your child. Therapy will help you maintain your relationship by taking some of the heat out of contact with your child, by showing you how to stay cool in the face of provocation and to keep your interactions positive and healthy.

Our purpose in conducting such a thorough evaluation is to make an accurate diagnosis—to give a name to the patient's problems so that we can select the proper treatment. Unfortunately, the psychiatrist's "bible," the *Diagnostic and*

Statistical Manual of Mental Disorders Third Edition, Revised (also known as the DSM-III-R), isn't very helpful in this regard. "Cult-itis" is not an officially recognized disorder. One diagnosis listed is a somewhat vague condition known as "atypical dissociative disorder." This broad label applies to people who experience a disturbance of identity, memory, or consciousness. As examples, the DSM-III-R mentions people who have been subjected to periods of prolonged and intense coercive persuasion (such as brainwashing, thought reform, or indoctrination while the captive of terrorists or cultists). That's all it says. There's no list of signs or symptoms, no list of criteria, no suggestions for psychological testing that would enable a psychiatrist to recognize the problems of cult involvement. Additionally, the DSM-III-R offers no suggestions on how to treat any condition. One reason we urge you to check out your doctor's credentials is to make sure you are dealing with someone who specializes in adolescent problems or, ideally, has a background in handling cult-related issues.

Depending on circumstances and the results of the evaluation, then, the psychiatrist will work with you to design a treatment strategy that addresses your specific needs. Fortunately there are many forms of effective therapy available that can be adapted to the problem of cult involvement. This is true even if your child refuses (or is unable) to leave the cult and participate in the process.

Individual therapy, for example, allows the cult member (or any member of the family) to talk with the professional on a one-to-one basis. During their conversation the psychiatrist will encourage this person to explore the different issues, to express and examine his or her feelings about what is happening. The tone of the therapy sessions is crucial. For the therapist to come on like a prosecutor—"You're in a cult; why?"—won't help. A teenager will simply consider anyone who adopts such a tone to be "the enemy"—one of "them." Instead, the therapist should be supportive and positive in order to establish a feeling of trust and mutual cooperation.

Group therapy brings people in similar circumstances together and gives them a chance to interact under the direction of a trained professional. In groups participants can share their experiences and get feedback from other people. Often patients feel that this feedback is more meaningful than any advice or suggestions the psychiatrist may give during individual sessions.

In *family therapy*, the therapist can observe how the individual members interact with each other. Participants get a chance to share feelings that they may never express at home. The goal is to uncover hidden problems or attitudes that may be thwarting the family's attempts to live together.

If the patient suffers from an underlying mental disorder, the use of *medications* can help. Of course, there is no "anti-cult" pill. But if we find that feelings of depression, for example, spurred a patient to seek relief by joining a cult, then the use of antidepressants may improve her mood and restore her self-esteem. Other medications may be used to treat conduct disorders, psychosis, schizophrenia, and so on. One advantage of such medications is that by relieving psychiatric symptoms they allow other forms of therapy, such as individual therapy, to work.

Hospitalization is an option when the adolescent is unable to control his behavior, if his behavior severely disrupts the family's ability to function, if he is unable to perform at school, on the job, or as a member of society, or if he is engaging in dangerous behavior (especially true for Satanic cults).

Actually, our experience has shown that it can be difficult to help a cult-involved adolescent outside the hospital. One reason is that joining a cult may be only a symptom of the kid's problems in dealing with the "real world"—his family, school, or society at large. Allowing the kid to remain in his usual environment may only perpetuate the problem. For example, he may leave the doctor's office only to go hang out with the same group of friends that encouraged his antisocial behavior in the first place. Similarly, asking him to come into therapy for an hour twice, three times, even five times a week may not be enough. An inpatient program offers constant, round-the-clock care; therapy can happen in a shorter time, with greater intensity, and with better results.

Another important benefit of inpatient treatment programs is that they provide an enormous amount of structure to the child's life. Every minute is planned. There are fixed mealtimes, classed with accredited teachers, individual and group therapy sessions, exercise programs, and structured entertainment periods. A system of rewards—increased privileges and freedoms—shows him the value of setting and reaching goals. Such discipline may be exactly what the teen was looking for when he joined the cult. There's wisdom in that old saying, "Idle hands are the devil's workshop"—a thought that's especially relevant to a discussion on cults. It's hard to get into mischief when you lead an active life. An intensive inpatient program shows a teen that structuring time results in healthy attitudes and gives him a big boost in his self-esteem.

There are some problems that may emerge during the therapeutic process. For one thing, people who leave cults may become fanatically anticult, as though purging their guilty feelings about having been a victim. One goal of therapy is to help people become more centered, to avoid such emotional and behavioral extremes. Conversely, in other cases, ex-members only want to forget what happened to them and will resist therapy that asks them to focus on the subject. The danger here is that suppressed feelings may erupt violently later, as a kind of delayed reaction. Also, at some point, work with the therapist must come to an end. When it does, people may experience the same kinds of feelings they did when divorcing themselves from the cult. Such feelings need to be dealt with.

At its best, psychiatric treatment offers patients a healthy, constructive, and effective way to pursue their quest for personal growth and insight—the same quest that may have led them to the cult in the first place.

Throughout this book our purpose has been to open your eyes: to show you how cults operate, to indicate the warning signs of cult involvement, and to provide you with some options for dealing with the problem. We have probably raised as many questions as we have answered; if so we encourage you to talk to your local librarian or mental health association, or get in touch with one of the cult support groups located across the country. Be assured that there are many sensitive, qualified people who understand what you are going through and can provide you with the help you need.

And remember, too, that the best defense against a cult is the parent's love for the child. Use that power well, and no cult—no matter how devious, no matter how compelling—will succeed.

Appendix

NATIONAL RESOURCES

American Family Foundation, PO Box 336, Westin, MA 02193—for an extensive list of publications.

Commission on Cults and Missionaries, Jewish Federation Council of Greater Los Angeles, 6505 Wilshire Blvd., Suite 802, Los Angeles, CA 90048, 213-852-1235 (ext. 2813)

Cult Awareness Network - National Office, 2421 West Pratt Blvd., Suite 1173, Chicago, IL 60645, 312-267-7777

Cult Clinic, Jewish Family Services of Los Angeles, 6505 Wilshire Blvd., Suite 608, Los Angeles, CA 90048, 213-852-1234 (ext. 2650)

Cult Project/Project Culte, 3460 Stanley Street, Montreal, Quebec H3A1R8, Canada

Task Force on Missionaries and Cults (and Cult Hotline/ Crisis Clinic), Jewish Community Relations Council of New York, 711 Third Avenue, 12th Floor, New York, NY 10017. Task Force: 212-983-4800, Hotline: 212-860-8533.

BIBLIOGRAPHY

Allen, C., and Metoyer, P.: "Crimes of the Occult," *Police*, February 1987.

Andres, R. and Lane, J.R.: *Cults and Consequences: The Definitive Handbook*. Los Angeles: Commission on Cults and Missionaries, Community Relations Committee, Jewish Federation Council of Greater Los Angeles, 1988.

Behar, R.: The Prophet and Profits of Scientology," *Forbes 400*, October 27, 1986.

Bordewich, F.M.: "Colorado's Thriving Cults," *New York Times Magazine*, May 1, 1988.

Bryant, J.: "Occult Crimes," *Police Marksman*, May/June 1987.

Enroth, R.: *A Guide to Cults and New Religions*. Downers Grove, IL: Inter-Varsity Press, 1983.

Galanter, M.: *Cults: Faith, Healing, and Coercion*. New York: Oxford University Press, 1989.

Galanter, M., ed: *Cults and New Religious Movements*. Washington, D.C.: American Psychiatric Association, 1989.

Green, M.: "A Boy's Love of Satan Ends in Murder, a Death Sentence—and Grisly Memories," *People*, December 1, 1986.

Halperin, D.A.: "Psychoanalysis and Cult Affiliation: Clinical Perspectives," *Cultic Studies Journal*, 1987.

Harris, M.P.: "Paradise Under Siege," *Time*, August 28, 1989.

Hubner, J., and Gruson, L.: "Dial Om for Murder," *Rolling Stone*, April 9, 1987.

Kandel, R.F.: "Litigating the Cult-Related Child Custody Case," *Cultic Studies Journal*, 1988.

Kelley, S.: "Ritualistic Abuse of Children: Dynamics and Impact," *Cultic Studies Journal*, 1988.

King, P.: "Heavy Metal Music and Drug Abuse in Adolescents," *Postgraduate Medicine*, April 1988.

Landa, S.: "Hidden Terror: Child Abuse in 'Religious' Sects and Cults," *Justice for Children*, Fall 1985.

Larson, B.: *Larson's Book of Cults*. Wheaton, IL: Tyndale House Publishers, Inc. 1982.

Levine, A.: "On the Trail of High Weirdness: Cults are on the Rise, But They're More Odd than Menacing," *U.S. News & World Report*, November 14, 1988.

Long, M.W.: "The Cult Appeal: Susceptibilities of the Missionary Kid," *Cultic Studies Journal*, 1987.

Lyons, A.: *Satan Wants You*. New York: The Mysterious Press, 1988.

Maron, N.: "Family Environment as a Factor in Vulnerability to Cult Involvement," *Cultic Studies Journal*, 1988.

Meeks, J.E.: *High Times/Low Times: The Many Faces of Adolescent Depression*. Summit, N.J.: The PIA Press, 1988.

Norris, J., and Potter, J.A.: "The Devil Made Me Do It," *Penthouse*, January 1986.

Reed, S.: "Anxious Mothers Battle a Therapy 'Cult' for Their Kids," *People*, July 25, 1988.

Ross, J.C., and Langone, M.D.: *Cults: What Parents Should Know*. Weston, Mass.: American Family Foundation, 1988.

Sirkin, M.I., and Grellong, B.A.: "Cult vs. Non-Cult Jewish Families: Factors Influencing Conversion," *Cultic Studies Journal*, 1988.

Solomon, A.O.: "Psychotherapy of a Casualty from a Mass Therapy Encounter Group: A Case Study," *Cultic Studies Journal*, 1988.

Underwood, B., and Underwood, B.: *Hostage to Heaven*, New York: Clarkson N. Potter, 1979.

Wedge, T.W., and Powers, R.L.: *The Satan Hunter.* Canton, Ohio: Daring Books, 1988.

INDEX

ABOUT THE AUTHORS....

Larry E. Dumont, M.D., is the Associate Director of the Adolescent Program at Fair Oaks Hospital in Summit, NJ. He has served as a Clinical Instructor in Psychiatry at both Tulane University School of Medicine and New York University School of Medicine. Dr. Dumont graduated Phi Beta Kappa from Tulane University and is an AOA graduate of the Northwestern University School of Medicine.

Richard I. Altesman, M.D., is the Medical Director of Stony Lodge Hospital in Briarcliff Manor, NY. Dr. Altesman, a graduate of the State University of New York, was a Fellow at Harvard's Massachusetts General Hospital and Resident in Psychiatry at Harvard's McLean Hospital, where he became Chief Resident in 1978. He was Director of Adult Services and Director of Medical Education at Fair Oaks Hospital in Summit, NJ before assuming his current position at Stony Lodge.